A Question
for Jesus

First published by O Books, 2009
O Books is an imprint of John Hunt Publishing Ltd., The Bothy, Deershot Lodge, Park Lane, Ropley,
Hants, SO24 0BE, UK
office1@o-books.net
www.o-books.net

Distribution in:

UK and Europe
Orca Book Services
orders@orcabookservices.co.uk
Tel: 01202 665432 Fax: 01202 666219
Int. code (44)

USA and Canada
NBN
custserv@nbnbooks.com
Tel: 1 800 462 6420 Fax: 1 800 338 4550

Australia and New Zealand
Brumby Books
sales@brumbybooks.com.au
Tel: 61 3 9761 5535 Fax: 61 3 9761 7095

Far East (offices in Singapore, Thailand,
Hong Kong, Taiwan)
Pansing Distribution Pte Ltd
kemal@pansing.com
Tel: 65 6319 9939 Fax: 65 6462 5761

South Africa
Alternative Books
altbook@peterhyde.co.za
Tel: 021 555 4027 Fax: 021 447 1430

Text copyright Tonika Rinar 2008

Design: Stuart Davies

ISBN: 978 1 84694 234 1

A CIP catalogue record for this book is available
from the British Library.

Printed by Digital Book Print

O Books operates a distinctive and ethical publishing philosophy in
all areas of its business, from its global network of authors to
production and worldwide distribution.
This book is produced on FSC certified stock, within ISO14001
standards. The printer plants sufficient trees each year through
the Woodland Trust to absorb the level of emitted carbon in
its production.

A Question for Jesus

Tonika Rinar

BOOKS

Winchester, UK
Washington, USA

CONTENTS

Dedication

This book is dedicated to everyone whoever.......asked.

The Early Years

Why You?

"Why do you think the Spirit of Jesus chose you?" I am often asked. The questioner silently studies my face, probes into my personality, and looks for any unseen clues that might give them the answer they seek. He or she asks about my lifestyle. They want to know my thoughts and opinions and my background. How I manage to be a wife and a mother to four children while running my clinic and doing this "cutting edge work" that I was born into doing?

Well, the simple answer is that I don't see that I was "chosen". In the earlier days, I surrendered to my destiny, a destiny which opened endless doorways and gave birth to a freedom within me, and connected me with the force we know as Universal Flow, God and Creation. Within this ultimate force, I was to meet and communicate with over 600 energies; energies that include Archangels and everyday type Angels, a freedom to travel through the Heavens/Astral Realms and, ultimately, for me to travel back in time to watch historical and biblical events that have molded our lives today. The profoundness of the information that was being channeled through me made me seriously think that the Universe had made a mistake in picking me.[1]

I thought I was an absolute daft choice! I felt flawed as my

---

1. Channeling - This was a process where my will stepped out of my body and a Universal Energy or Spirit entered to utilize my body to move and communicate using my vocal cords and limbs. My head is gently pulled back, as the energy enters into my body, then my head is gently straightened. The transformation is complete, the sound of the voice changes, and an entirely new personality and aura is projected, as their unique mannerisms, expressions and wisdom takes control and utilizes my body.

education had been cut short and I wasn't someone who had spent years studying psychic phenomena nor was I on a search for "enlightenment". To sleep peacefully at night was all that I desired.

The intent that governed my way of living were to: 1) always respect those around me, 2) never be hurtful, 3) see the best in everyone and every situation, 4) live a truthful life, and, 5) not worry about anything that can't be put in your coffin! So having the Universe open this doorway within me to experience the inner core and Spirit of Creation/God led me to wonder as to how to integrate this awakening into my normal everyday living. Needless to say, I struggled in a major way. I just felt that the information and experiences were wasted on me. I wasn't consciously *looking* for answers to life. I already had concluded that religions had too many contradictions in their way of teaching. To me, God/Creation is in and all around every particle in the Universe. This life creating force has provided us with an independence to think, feel, learn and expand. It has enabled a deep compassion within us all (a compassion that ignites our integrity to what many of us see as "right or wrong"). My confusion therefore was; why after providing us with such independence would this force then (as some belief systems would have us believe) sit in judgment of us? My struggle led me to think I must be crazy! The Universe I felt would have done better to have picked someone who was perhaps a touch more enlightened.

I met Adrian a few months into my "Awakening". He did his best to reassure me that there was absolutely nothing wrong with me. "You are in denial of yourself," he would say. I wasn't convinced. So, I went to see a parapsychologist in the hope that I would be declared insane. Then, I would not have to be too concerned that the Universe had got it wrong. At least I'd have an answer; an answer that could help me to understand that part of me was actually mad and I could deal with that part accordingly.

Not quite knowing what to make of everything that was

happening to me, the parapsychologist declared me perfectly sane and "one of the most psychic people she had met". I should have been pleased. I thought, *Darn! Now I don't have an excuse to stop the Universal connections that were coming through.* I still struggled with the understanding as to how I was capable of receiving such life challenging and transforming insights. At least I had the comfort of knowing I wasn't insane!

Growing up

Both my father and mother were refugees from Czechoslovakia and granted asylum by the British Government in the early 1950s. My brother and I were born soon after they settled here. I was 6-months old when my mother died suddenly of a fatal blood clot to the brain.

Having no family to help my father bring up his children, he was left with no choice other than to put us into state care. I stayed until the age of 4 years. My brother was 2 years older and was sent to a different children's home. My father visited us both fortnightly.

I remember a boy who was of similar age. He had been placed in the same home as me because his mother had to work fulltime. She had been abandoned by her husband when she was pregnant. She had family, but they did not provide her adequate support. She and my father married. I don't think it was a great love they shared, but it was a convenient friendship which enabled them both to create a family unit for her child, my brother and me.

My education was not completed because, at the age of 15 years and 3 months, I had to leave school and start contributing financially to the upkeep of the home.

My first job was a junior office clerk for a large retailer. This job was very dull. The abrupt and premature ending of my education left me without a choice of career options, quite simply I had to take what was available. Eighteen months in an office job filing documents allowed me to mentally explore other work

possibilities. I finally concluded that hairdressing was the way
forward for me. The problem was that training took 3 years
working in a salon as a trainee hairstylist and the pay was much
lower than that of an office clerk. The only way I could embark on
my chosen career was to find a job that paid a higher salary. The
extra money could be used to pay for a private nine-month
intensive course and cover my living expenses at home. I soon
found one as a sales assistant. Three years later I was able to start
my course, passing with one of the highest marks, I began my
career working in one of London's top hair salons, where I
continued to learn and practice my trade.

I married my first husband before I was 25 years old. We got
along well together, but I did not love him. I had not received love
as a child; so therefore, I concluded that real love was as rare as a
diamond and that an element of luck was needed to meet
someone who cared as much for you as you did for them. Even
being blessed with children was something I felt would elude me.
So for me, love was a fantasy that was designated to the pages of
romantic novels. I never dared to believe that I would be so lucky
to find true love.

In many ways, this skepticism of mine contradicted the deep
compassion I felt for people who were suffering on this Earth
through famine, wars, or domestic violence. Throughout my
childhood I spent every night praying with passion. Given the
pain that I had in my heart for these people, I wanted their
suffering to cease. I truly could not understand the nature of
mans' greed and aggression.

My childhood was not a happy time, the insecurities of my
stepmother began to manifest into a negative and an unstable way
of living. Fortunately, I was and remain blessed with an innate
sense of "not taking people's anger or aggression personally." This
was especially useful when living and dealing with my
stepmother. She was for much of the time emotionally unstable
and angry, which made it virtually impossible to relax at home.

Often my brother and I were the projected targets of her anger and physical aggression, even as a young child I was capable of being objective to her anger and not take her behavior personally. I could see her torment and struggle in trying to be what society expected her to be. Now as an adult, when I look back upon my somewhat "colorful upbringing", I can see that such an innate sense was the saving grace of my emotional psyche during such a vulnerable age!

Throughout the traumatic years of my childhood I would find solace in nature. Here I could see and feel the magic of life. It was in this free and abundant magic of nature that I came alive. I would question the contradictions brought on by religious teachings of "God and his final judgment".

How can a God that is supposed to be all loving, a God that creates the most wonderful summer days that are filled with air blissfully warm to the body, a God that produces flowers unique in their diversity to each other, flowers that give us the sense of smell so we can fill our Spirit with the perfume they so freely offer, a God that has given us eyes to see the way the wind appears to create random dances on everything it touches, a God that gives us a heart to feel this magic, a God that can sculpt the most intricate of patterns in a single snowflake, leaves us to suffer. The perception that God leaves us to struggle through wars and famines, and when death arrives and judgment day finally comes we are to be judged on our life's activities, places a lot of fear into people. Such beliefs contradicted the God I saw all around me.

But, Why You?

The conclusion I have so far reached to the question: Why I am able to communicate in such a unique way with all in Creation? Is possibly due to two factors, namely; my non-acceptance of the conventional understanding of the energy we call God, along with an innate knowing, feeling and appreciation of this infinite fundamental energy that flows through all of life (through everyone and everything). It is these two things which I believe has enabled me to expand my consciousness beyond humankind's current restricting reasoning, expected limitations and judgment.

Stepping into Destiny

My awakening and surrender to the flow of the Universe was at a time when the fight within me had reached a crossroads, and a choice had to be made. Either I stepped into my destiny and do what I was created to do or "burn out" completely. Intuitively I knew there was a greater part of me which I continued to deny. It was a part that really scared me. At this crossroads, I reached two paths. One path I knew, the other was unknown. I made the conscious choice to take the unknown path, since I was aware that to continue to live in the same way (walking the same path) was a direction of self-denial that would probably lead to an early physical departure from this planet!

One month into this "awakening" my husband and I agreed our common interest in life was our friendship that had died years earlier. We made the decision to divorce, leaving me with full responsibility of my three children who were aged 10 months, four years, and seven years old. My now ex-husband decided to create a new life. Over the months he saw less and less of the children. Once he remarried, his new life did not include them. This appeared not to concern the children as for most of their short lives their father was not around. The children adapted to these changes with ease.

My children expanded the magic I saw in the Universe. I marveled at the way their seductive innocence created a world that I could escape into. My life with them took me away from the many mundane pressures of every day living. It would be in their world that I naturally felt centered and re-energized. I was continually amazed that I should be so lucky that they were in my life. I felt so happy. My "awakening" had spiritually opened me to a great sense of fulfillment *and* to be blessed with three fine and unique little characters, it was more than I would ever dare to hope for. I felt I had everything, yet without searching, the Universe, God and Creation was soon to bring me a very special man who was to become my life partner and friend. This man ignited within me the love that really can exist between two people.

Adrian became husband to me and father to my three children. Four years later, I gave birth to our fourth child, a little girl. Life was exceptionally good. I was humbled joyfully at the way my life had completely turned around. Adrian was a great mate. He had a passion and an inner drive to find the truth in *everything* in Creation. His loving support and encouragement of the channeling taking place enabled my confidence to grow, which allowed my "Awakening" to expand even further.

Meeting the Spirit of Jesus

My "channeling" (or as I prefer to call it "lending my body") had begun in March 1991. Fifteen months had now passed, during which time I had experienced many wonderful communications with different aspects and energies of Creation. I had come to realize that absolutely everything in Creation had a consciousness and their own unique personality. Literally everything; the Sun, the Stars, the Earth, the Moon, archetypes of animals, various "mythological creatures" such as Pegasus and Unicorns, the God and Goddess energies attributed to various cultures of Greece, Egypt and India – Zeus, Apollo, Isis, Thoth, Kali and Genesha, Angels and Archangels – Uriel and Michael and many, many, many more came to introduce themselves to me and share their insights as to their particular role and existence within the great universal energy that some people term God.

Approximately 200 such communications had taken place and I was now becoming increasingly experienced at working and communicating with these wonderful pure light energies. None of these energies had ever lived a physical life on earth, they had never incarnated. It was therefore most unexpected that during one particular session the Spirit of Jesus began to communicate through me. This was the beginning of what eventually became a series of channeled sessions with the Spirit of Jesus, over a 16-year period. He shared a greater understanding of his earthly life, his teachings and his ultimate Soul purpose.

Around six people would be invited to participate in these sessions. Although it was hoped that Jesus would come to communicate with us, it was never expected by me or the group of people present. Whoever came to communicate with the group was welcomed and questions would be asked to whichever Universal Energy was "borrowing" my body at that time.

The particular Universal Energy would enter into me once I had mentally gone through my process of *discernment* (the culmination of this process being my absolute surrender to Universal Flow and Truth). My blood and bones would be filled with a particular sensation that my mind could not mimic, confirming to me that I was at that moment fully connected to Divine Will / God. My consciousness and my will gently moves into the "back seat" of my awareness, enabling observation and sensation within all my cells. This is great as I see and feel the deepest memories and thoughts from whichever Energy, Being or Spirit is using my body to communicate at the time. This flexibility within my persona is brilliant as I can later relay all that I experienced during the "channeling" session to the sitter/s and with you, the reader.

It was during my early channeling experiences that I very quickly learnt how the mind can unwittingly deceive, telling you that you are connected to a Divine Source, that you are coming from a pure place, together with many other reassuring deceptive thought forms which come from the mind and the ego when "opening" oneself up to the Universe. However, the blood and the bones do not have the ability to declare an untruth and so I would wait for a particular sensation in them which confirmed to me that

I was fully connected to Divine Will. Experience has taught me that simply asking for spiritual protection does not mean you necessarily get it! Quite simply, if you are about to allow your consciousness to take a back seat, symbolically speaking, there ought not to be any unconscious wants, needs and desires lurking deep within the psyche that becomes "bait" to attract negative Energies who are not who they say they are! [2]

This process of Universal connection does not allow me to influence who or which particular Spirit or Universal Energy comes to communicate. The Universe will only ever "send" to my body the relevant Energy that was to expand these "channeled" sessions further. Needless to say, my confidence in the power of Universal Timing grew immensely.

My apprenticeship into the workings of the Universe (and all things spiritual) was entirely undertaken by the Universal Flow/ God/ Creation and the Beings and Energies that exist within this wonderful energy.

---

2. For more information on discernment and the mind see 'Journey Home – A True Story of Time and Inter-dimensional Travel'- T. Rinar.

2

Jesus Enters

"I taught of life and of how there is no separation within
man and God,
And still man cannot fully understand this very simplest
of teachings".

One morning in May 1992, a man who was studying theology and had made this his life's work, came to see me and asked if he could have a personal "channeled" session. Agreeing to this, informing him that, "I do not make a request for any particular Energy/Entity to 'come through' as this type of request puts limitations on the Universal Flow, which can draw in Energies/Entities who are not who they say they are". I made him aware that it was possible that nothing may happen and that we would have to accept that a communication was not meant to be on this occasion. My surrender to Universal Flow was founded upon; a trust that Creation / God knew when and how to expand our consciousness, and an acceptance of the information shared by whichever Being/ Energy the Universe deemed relevant to send to communicate. Understanding this, our session began.

I went through my process of discernment and surrender. Immediately, my blood and bones responded. However, this time the sensation I experienced was hugely magnified, calming quickly any residue of internal doubts that had become part of my nature.

My head was gently pulled back and twisted from side to side as my consciousness eased out, ready for observation. Unaware of who was about to enter, my body took a deep breath as if to guide this Spirit into my physical form. Firmly and slowly the connecting Energy/Spirit brought my head back to its normal position. Usually, within 30 seconds or so the Energy/Spirit has become accustomed to the workings of my body and (through the use of my vocal cords) introduces themselves to all those present.

On this occasion the Spirit who entered was taking a considerable time to explore the feeling of being in a body. My body felt extremely familiar to this Spirit. It was through the Spirit's remembrance of the physical form that made me realize this Spirit had once had a physical life here on Earth. Wow! I thought, wondering with excitement as to who this could be, at the same time feeling slightly nervous as this type of connection was a first for me. I had become so used to "channeling" Energies, Entities and Spirits that had never incarnated on Earth, so there was a sense of not knowing how this communication was going to progress. I understood that everything was as it universally should be, for my blood and bones responded excitedly at the point of my surrender. I relaxed and became filled with a sense of curiosity as I fully surrendered my body to this Energy.

I wondered if this Spirit could sense the air of anticipation that was filling the room as both I and the theology student waited for the first spoken words from this Spirit; the words that would tell us who was now in our presence.

Whether this Spirit was aware or not of my growing excitement eluded me. The Spirit was all-encompassed in the memory of physical life and was not going to be rushed. Realizing this, I succumbed to the timing of this Spirit.

My body was immersed in wonderment and joy as this Spirit gently lifted my right hand to my face and very tenderly touched my cheek. In doing so, the Spirit recalled through its essence the memory of what it felt like to touch and be touched. A sense of incredible joy swept through the very essence of this Spirit as my hand was then raised to my head. The Spirit softly fingered my hair, remembering its sensation and texture, whilst recalling the memories of their own physical form during their previous life on earth.

The Spirit slowly lowered my head, empowered in familiar remembrance and awe of the creation of the human form. Raising my head to face the sitter, the Spirit bowed in acknowledgement of the person with whom the Spirit had come to speak and placed his hand upon my chest, touching my heart in acknowledgement of my essence. Taking a gentle breath in, the Spirit spoke....

Jesus: "I am the Master Jesus and I welcome your being into my heart. My physical vibration when I walked this planet was known to many as Yeshua. But, many know my life's vibration as Jesus, some refer to my energy as the Master Jesus. I come in joy and in light and I come in call to you. You may ask."

Whoa! I felt as if a "jolt" had swept through my consciousness. I was stunned, Shocked, almost swept away with emotion!! Feeling in awe to have such a pure being in my body. Sensing my whirling emotions Jesus' essence heightened in strength, creating calmness within me, as the session began........

Question: I have some questions that I would like to ask about your lifetime on Earth, and what I most want to know is; what it was that you wanted to teach?

Jesus: My child, there has been very little if any progress since my incarnation on this planet. I taught of life and of how there is no separation within man and God; and still man cannot fully understand this very simplest of teachings. When I walked on the earth plane I was shunned by many and this is because man was fearing to move and acknowledge his true being.

The guilt man held within his Soul, he chose to hold and not release, so I was placed by many on a platform. I was placed higher than the person who I walked with. I was placed only like this by those who chose to follow their path of guilt. For them enlightenment was too bright, they only could see the dark. So by placing my being higher than their own they chose to proclaim that I was a dictator.

Many writings have been written of my existence and many have been written by the mind, how the mind of mankind chose to see and not with the heart. When I walked on the earth plane I walked **with** man and I walked **as** man - no greater, no lesser.

I came to show man how he is a true being of light; and many of the so-called miracles that I seemingly performed were only because of the energy that was shared by myself and my fellow beings.

Question: There is a story that with a small number of loaves and fishes, you fed a large number of people. Can you explain how that came about?

Jesus: This my child was not so. This has already been made by the mind of man to make my being greater than his own. What actually occurred on that day was much, much teaching to the understanding of love for all. Everyone who experienced this understanding was nourished by love. Love within themselves and the love that emanated from their neighbor. The loaves and fishes were used as an example and explained to people who could not understand this most natural of phenomena of love. As you share to your neighbor, you are blessed also with the sharing of your neighbor to you, and so are nurtured throughout your being.

For, in the first and beyond is my Father, is your Father, is the Creator, is the Source, is the One, is All. And when a child fully acknowledges this energy within their being they are nourished accordingly, because at that point there is no separation.

I was **not** a magician. For much has been implicated that I was. For how can any being materialize enough physical food to feed a multitude.

I am no greater, no lesser, I am as you.

Question: There are many stories of healing - that you healed. Did this occur?

Jesus: Much of this did occur, but it was also the being who healed himself by acknowledging the Creator in his Soul. I merely could become a channel to open the heart of the child in question so they could also experience total oneness. Yes, much occurred, but it came because the child was willing.

Question: Did you send your disciples - your closest associates - out to preach and to heal at any time?

Jesus: At this point I must tell you very firmly that my disciples were not as is spoken *(as has been written)*. Yes, I had around me very close beings but also I had the love of many children with whom I talked and with everyone with whom I spoke. Each being became also a disciple, but not a disciple of mine but of their own path.

You also are a disciple but for your own enlightenment. No one can teach you - only yourself.

Much will be made clearer as you begin to understand this. I also can tell you that the close ones around me - not all, but many - began to preach, as you say, but much ego entered. So, my very simple teachings were lost.

I also had ego. So you see, I am no greater and no lesser. I feel the love that each man feels within his heart

Question: In the stories that come down, there is somebody known as John the Baptist. Is this somebody that you knew?

Jesus: This, my child was so. John, as he was known, was indeed a very pure Soul. Much also has been written of him and much has been out of context.

There is silence as the sitter takes in the reply to his question. Jesus leans slightly forward and gently asks......

You are feeling somewhat confused?

The silence continues, with compassion to the sitter Jesus

explains......

My child, I walked the Earth, I too know of confusion. For many times I experienced this confusion. I was a man also. But, there is no confusion in the heart, for in each heart is the seed of all Creation.

I sensed from Jesus' Spirit that in telling the sitter that the stories of John the Baptist were written out of context (false writings) had caused him to feel confused.

Question: There is a story that you were in the wilderness for forty days and were tempted by the Devil. Can you tell me what actually happened?

Jesus: This for me was a very dark time. I had felt abandoned by my Father *(God)* as many children do today. And it was through this abandoned feeling that I experienced that confusion. Yes, I was tempted.

I was tempted to go back into the place where my brothers, my fellow man, dwelt. I was tempted to become glorified, and yes the temptation was very strong. For this occurred simply because I had felt I had been abandoned by my Father, the Creator.

But what I had chosen for myself was to separate my being from my Father and this is when the temptation occurred. It was for me very dark.

Jesus' memory of those times were of isolation, feeling lost and pulled in many directions. He was confused and did not know his true self.

Question: Was it after this period that you began teaching?

Jesus: I had been teaching, more I had been **sharing** I think is a finer way to describe my work.

I had been sharing since I can remember, but I had chosen to be alone for this time *(the 40 days)* because I knew my ego was becoming quite potent and I knew this was not to be.

My ego was becoming large because many flocked to hear me talk. So, it was always very difficult for me to find solitude, so I chose to be alone for this time. My ego was telling me I can do this without my Father, and my heart was telling me no!

Question: It is reported that when you were on the cross you said; "My God, My God, why hast thou forsaken me?"

Jesus shakes my right hand vigorously across chest and raises it up high and outwards, this was to prevent the Biblical quote from entering his Spirit. This action stopped the energy of the quote in mid-air.

Jesus' was without verbal response and his Spirit held absolute no acknowledgement of this person's question. I had witnessed, felt and understood in an instance that truth does not need defense or justification. Truth just is.

The sitter not understanding Jesus' lack of acknowledgement to his question probed deeper......

Questioner: It didn't happen?
Jesus pauses, then firmly responds…
Jesus: I choose not to acknowledge this.

If Jesus had given an answer to this question and denied these words, then power would have been given to the falseness of them. Many times during channeling sessions I have observed how Universal Energies / Beings working to assist mankind to grow and expand in truth and oneness, will never acknowledge an untruth that has often been written for dramatic effect. Such an untruth acts as a stumbling-block for expansions in awareness and truth.

My thoughts…..

When thinking about Jesus' life rationally: Jesus had already spent 40 days in the wilderness struggling with his ego which had ultimately caused him to feel separated from God. Once he returned from the wilderness Jesus had triumphed over his ego and so there was no longer a place in his being that was separate from God. Why would he then announce to everyone during the last moments of his life that "God had forsaken him?" Symbolically speaking, once you have taken your first

breath of life will you then later forget how to breath and then announce
to the world that air no longer exists? It didn't happen!

Question: As the story comes down, it seems as if you could have
avoided death on the cross, by not being in Jerusalem at that time.
So it looks as if that is what you chose to do. Is that correct?
Jesus: This, *(referring to his death)* my child was my ultimate task.
This had to occur for the Christ Energy to be grounded into the
hearts of man.

When the Christ Energy (or the Christ Light as some term this
energy) first communicated with me, I had such a sense of awe. I had
assumed that the Christ Energy and Jesus were the same essence. For
over a year I worked with this wonderful healing energy. Not once did I
think of asking for clarification that the Christ Energy was the essence
of Jesus? The Christ Energy would assist me in my treatment of people
suffering injuries and illness, with remarkable outcomes. This very pure
Energy would guide me to blockages or reveal to me where disease was
occurring in a patient's body or aura. It was only much later when I
started to communicate with the Spirit of Jesus that I realized there was
a very clear difference of vibration and density between Jesus and the
Christ Energy.

As Jesus explained his ultimate task was to ground the Christ
Energy into this dimension and into our hearts. Many people wonder as
to their purpose in life. Indeed of all my communications with Jesus,
never once did I feel he knew his purpose. (Jesus' purpose, it seems,
became clear to his Spirit once he had departed from his physical body).
What Jesus did have, and I could often feel this, was his strong sense of
conviction and direction, (apart from his dark time when he took himself
off to the wilderness to allow himself time for clarity over his ego).

His body was a conduit for the Christ Energy to ignite on to this
planet. His love and selfless sacrifice enabled the successful grounding
of the Christ Energy.

This Christ Energy pulsated through the Earth, in a similar way that
electricity pulsates through a cable. Electricity may flow freely through

a cable, but a plug is required to receive the power generated by the electricity - it doesn't just manifest.

Jesus, symbolically speaking, was the human "plug" that allowed the Christ Energy to enter onto the Earth. Jesus, by living his life and triumphing over his own internal demons, enabled his Spirit to be completely clear of restrictions and limitations. This was especially true at the point of his physical death, allowing the Christ Energy total freedom to enter into this dimension, into the Earth. He was indeed an extremely clear " plug"!

How the Christ Energy and Jesus Differed

When I experience the Christ Energy there is a strength and sense of oldness connected to it which leads me to surmise that this energy was well established by God, Creation and Universal Flow (using Earthly timing) long before the life of Jesus. I experience a singular vibration and color emanating from the Christ Energy, and is a considerable contrast to the energy of the Spirit of Jesus.

The Christ Energy (a very pure healing and transformational energy) feels to be one specific aspect of God / Creation. To clarify; God Creation has an incomprehensible amount of vibrations and colors.

In contrast, Jesus' energy seems more in tune with the energy of mankind (which contains many vibrations and colors). Jesus' Spirit is aware that our wants and desires create blocks in our common psyche whether the blocks be individual or collective. These are blocks that prevent the power of Creation to work smoothly through us and within us. Jesus' Spirit knows the joys of living, he knows the magic and wonderment of life, and he truly knows the struggle and pain we all experience.

Jesus continues......

Jesus: Do you have any more questions? There is much, ask? *Indicating to the sitter to feel free to carry on.*

Question: The story is that you went to the Temple and drove out the people who were there changing money - did this happen?

Jesus answers, passion directs his words …..

Jesus: Oh, this happened not only once, this happened many, many, many times, many times. And I can also tell you, not only did I shout, I also physically threw these beings out. But I also acknowledged that, although they were somewhat unenlightened, *(the traders)* I knew through my anger their hearts had been touched, for they knew this was wrong. This happened often.

Temples and such were often treated as if they were market places and through all this the only emotion that filled my Father's house was greed.

Question: It is said that you used the expression, "The Kingdom of Heaven" at times. What did that mean? What did you want people to understand by that?

Jesus: The Kingdom of Heaven is the Soul of the Heart, quite simply. For man to enter the Kingdom of Heaven - the Soul of the heart - he must first find peace within and without; for when this has been achieved, he has found the Kingdom of Heaven.

Question: The Jewish people at that time were expecting and awaiting a Messiah.

Was that a misunderstanding on their part?

Jesus: As there is today, much has been written of the second coming of Christ. But what this is, is the Christ Energy being acknowledged within all peoples of your planet. This is, in fact, the second coming. For man has long looked for another being to show him out of darkness, but the step must come from within.

As Jesus explained the second coming, the Christ Energy being acknowledged within all peoples, I could clearly sense the title Christ Energy is the name given to what is the energy of awakening. (The Christ Energy being the name that this awakening energy has been given in the western world and therefore this same awakening energy may be given a different title, as spiritual awakening occurs, in other regions of the world - which have other dominant belief systems).

Question: It is said that you taught people that the Kingdom of Heaven is at hand and the way that is translated, it is not clear whether you mean it is something that will happen very soon, or something that is happening right now. Which is it?

Jesus: The Kingdom of Heaven is the Soul of the Heart and it has always been there within each being, for each being must find peace to enter into the Kingdom of Heaven, the Soul of the Heart, and it is at hand because it dwells within each being.

But always man searches outwardly and not inwardly.

For first to acknowledge your perfection, your oneness with the Creator, when you have fully acknowledged this within your heart, then you are in the Soul of the Heart. But always ego fights.

The Kingdom of Heaven is not separate. Nothing is separate; everything is as one. And this I shared also with many people when I walked the planet. But you see how it has become misread because man has still to acknowledge his true perfection.

Question: Shortly before you left the planet, there was an event known as the last supper, when you took, perhaps, the Passover Feast with a few of your closest friends. And, from the events that happened, there has come down an account that has been given very great significance in services and in liturgy. Can you tell us what did happen at that meal together?

Jesus: At this meal there was much distress and much anger towards many, many misled Souls *(referring to his persecutors).* At this supper my heart inside was bleeding for the pain of man.

The pain of man that Jesus refers to is the pain caused by mans' mental and emotional anguish. Observing and feeling Jesus' memory as he recalled the events of the last supper with his friends his whole essence was racked by the turmoil of mans' inner sufferings, thus resulting in acts filled with hatred and violation to their fellow man. Jesus continues........

This is most important (*said calmly and with firm precision*).

I will speak;

Wine was given by my being to calm the fear that was felt in the hearts of my friends, for it was not for me to depart from this planet in a cloud of fear. So when wine is given it is to release fear, and the wine is symbolic of the love that I felt as my heart bled for mankind. This, my child, is so important; it has through many, many, many, many, many ages been misread. But this is why I gave the wine: had there not been fear, then I would have not given the wine. It was so important to calm my friends; they were becoming very rowdy and were also plotting my release. Do you see?

Question: Plotting your release...?
Jesus: From my impending departure. But, it was time for my task to be completed on this planet.

Question: So, it has come down as being a very important event....
Jesus: It was, but not as many have seen it to be.

Question: And did you break bread and share it amongst them and did that have any particular significance?
Jesus: This was only because they drank too much wine. No more, it has no significance - only the wine.

As Jesus' Spirit recalled the events of this final gathering with his friends, I could see and feel his memory travel back to this time. Jesus had wanted to call his friends together to reassure them he would be okay and for them to remember how strong they were when they did not walk the path of fear. He felt a number of these friends (disciples) were, due to the fear that was manifesting through them, beginning to lose sight of the inner strength and freedom they had ignited within themselves.

Not all the friends were becoming fearfully anxious, three, (four including Judas) remained calm and of understanding of the unknown conviction that filled Jesus in his determination "not to renounce his belief"- a request that had been made by the authorities - in order to save himself.

Jesus' "stubbornness" (as the authorities deemed him to be) was to be his downfall. His fearful friends present at the supper felt Jesus was being stubborn and should be more "compromising" in his conviction in order to appease the authorities and diffuse the "outrage" that was going on. Jesus' friends knew he would not become quiet in his beliefs. But, they hoped they could placate him sufficiently enough so that he may listen to their "voice of reason". There was a suggestion to Jesus from some of his friends that the teachings could carry on, but in a "quieter" fashion and so not draw too much attention to himself. Jesus knew, by the reaction from them to his impending death, that they had not fully understood in their Spirit's, the Eternal Life, Power and Love of God. He knew they would understand more after his death. Jesus' entire being was filled with care and unconditional love in assisting his friends to strengthen their own Spirits. He reassured them and conversed with them for many hours.

Jesus continued....

Jesus: You may ask of me one more question for now. I will come again when the time is right.

Question: I have many more questions, but one in particular. It refers to a man called Paul, who, after you had physically left this planet, taught many people in your name. What he taught...

Jesus brushes hand back and forth in front of face. This response from Jesus was to not acknowledge the writings of Paul, as they were not completely true of his life and his words.

Jesus continues....

Jesus: This was not in my name. My name was misused. For what occurred when I left the planet was that much light came on the earth as many began to acknowledge the Christ energy within their being. And so, it was felt my name would be good to be used to attract many, but this was wrong.

Much confusion occurred after this time. You may carry on.

Encouraging one last question as the previous one was not relevant to his life.

Question: Most of the questions that I would ask at this time, you have already answered in some way or another. Thank you.

As a final question, I would like to ask if I was there at that time?

Responding tenderly and Jesus' Spirit opening to the heart of the sitter, he answered:

Jesus: You, my child, were in fact one of the soldiers escorting me up to the mount; but in your eyes I saw your compassion. I saw your great desire to acknowledge fully my existence. I saw in you much pain on behalf of many and I can tell you, my child, the pain that you felt was the pain also you carried for mankind.

So now, I will depart, and I can tell you, my child, it is by no coincidence that you are here. For many incarnations you have wanted the truth to be told. You knew there was much untruth being taught of my being and this is why we meet tonight.

From Jesus' memory I saw the face of this soldier, whose eyes filled with pain. The soldier, looking in the face of Jesus, lowered his gaze ashamed at the wronging of such a fine man, who he saw was both charismatic and passionate and was without hatred or malice. A man who despite suffering much physical pain and humiliation, emanated a purity that spoke directly to the soldier's heart - a heart that had been hardened by years of military service.

In acknowledgement of the sitters previous life as that soldier, so long ago, and for his now current life's search for truth, a search which had enabled Jesus' Spirit to converse with him; and in doing so release

Jesus' essence from the burden of falseness that had surrounded his being for such a long time. Jesus bowed low and then he informed the sitter....

Jesus: I will come again.

The Following Year
During the following months an enormous expansion within my Spirit occurred. My cells filled with new life, revealing the unlimited potential of mankind, that Jesus' words ignited within me. I was immersed in a sense of wonder of how the Universe / God had brought Jesus' Spirit to my psyche, to communicate through me and voice details of his life here on Earth. Jesus' life was no longer some written tale of long ago. My psyche had been allowed to explore, touch and sense Jesus' personality and the emotions he felt during his earthly existence. I was amazed by the unlimited possibilities the Universe presents to us.

Jesus' last words "I will come again" resounded through me. When and where was this to take place? Intuitively I was aware that there was still much more to be revealed about his life. My concern was whether I would allow sufficient freedom in my persona to fit into Universal timing and be receptive enough to allow another opportunity for Jesus to communicate through me.

After all, my concerns appeared genuine. My life is filled with similar day-to-day stresses that most people experience. One could argue that meditation was the best way to calm these man-made stresses. But, meditation was not for me, for my whole life is a meditation, and such a precious gift is life that I do not want to miss any waking moment of it. At the time of my first meeting with Jesus my children were eight, five and eighteen months old respectively (my fourth child was to be conceived a few years later). My greatest pleasure was seeing the smiles on the faces of my children, to sense the joy of life which they emanated rejuvenated me immensely. Being with my children made me feel complete. I was fulfilled and did not consciously desire or seem to require anything more in my life. The last thing I could have possibly expected was to be able to communicate with Jesus. Always questioning the Universe working through me with what I felt was a mammoth task. For I am a simple mother who had no particular interest in Jesus' life and little knowledge of world religions. In my heart I know the magical way the Universe works. But, my doubting side was convinced the Universe / Creation had got it seriously wrong in allowing Jesus to talk through me and to give such a personal and detailed account of his life.

My challenge it appeared, was to get out of my own self-doubting way and allow the Universe to flow in freedom through me. This was to be a momentous challenge, one on many occasions I thought I would never achieve. I tackled this challenge step by step. Many times I fell - some more painful than others. During this journey I was to have other meetings with Jesus' Spirit who shared many additional details and intimacies of his life.

3

The Second Meeting

"Your thoughts and your heart as one,
perfectly balanced, will bring you light."

This meeting involved six people whose paths had for a short while brought them into my life for this planned session with Jesus. These people were enthralled with the possibility of being in the presence of a truly great Spirit, excited to ask Jesus questions about his life; and brought questions to the meeting which stemmed from their individual perspectives' of his time on Earth.

This second meeting occurred around a year after the first. Intuitively, I had been aware for some weeks before that a second opportunity to communicate with Jesus would soon be possible. Timing for this meeting was made clear by the Universe instilling calmness in my ever self-doubting psyche! My personal struggle to accept myself is replaced with a feeling of excitement that reverberates through my mental and emotional levels. I am filled with ease and a sense of support. It is this obvious and altered recognizable feeling of change within my mental and emotional self that determines when to hold a session. A date was set for us all to meet in my home. My children were to be looked after by a kind neighbor for the two-hour meeting.

The intention behind our gathering was to have the opportunity to communicate with Jesus' Spirit. However, within me and the entire group was an openness to accept fully whichever Spirit or Energy the Universe sent to talk with us. Such a flexibility enabled the Universe to flow freely and to absolute truth; it was the key intent and grounding that was to create an expansion within mankind and the Universe.

Welcoming the group and observing that everyone was seated comfortably, I sat on my large cushion on the floor. Sitting close to the ground was more comfortable for me to "channel", than sitting comfortably on a soft armchair.

I began with my process of discernment before allowing my will to step aside and my body to be surrendered to the Universe. Three or four minutes later my body filled with a familiar essence, as Jesus' Spirit entered. Taking a few moments to feel the sensation of being once more back in a physical body, whilst simultaneously recognizing the familiarity of my physical structure; the Spirit raised my head and used my hand to touch my heart - whilst bowing to the group in acknowledgement of them......

Group: Welcome.
Jesus: I am the energy, the Soul, the one known to you all as the Master Jesus.

Question: Welcome, thank you for coming tonight.
Jesus: I have come here in the most sacred of moments to bring clarity to any words you may wish to share. I ask that you feel not uncertain but open your hearts, for it is the openness in your hearts that has brought you here tonight.

Jesus felt an uncertainty within the group, a hesitation from some of them as to how to begin to feel at ease enough to ask questions that may appear too personal or insignificant. Jesus' words gave the group assurance to ask whatever they individually felt was relevant.

Question: Master Jesus, how do you feel about how you are perceived today on Earth?
Jesus: To answer your words would cause much pain within the hearts of many. I can tell you all *(of)* my true essence, NOT that which is written in books, for these are man's ideals. I can share

with you the way I would share with a brother. I would ask that mankind, all the peoples of this planet, would see me only as their brother. But unfortunately I am in many houses revered. This causes much separation. My life was to teach there is no separation and yet in many "houses", reverence is the most great of all separation for it allows no true connection between brothers.[3]

Question: Jesus, when you were growing up on Earth, did you have the same struggle to find your light that we are having as humans?

Jesus: In answer to your most potent question, I must give my words which were:

This is so *(Yes)*. Many, many beings could not see the inner struggle that occurred within my Soul.

There was much darkness upon the planet and when one always walks in darkness, it is often so, so hard to find light. So, one begins to question oneself. But by always questioning oneself and not taking oneself for granted, then the clarity comes........ from within! For the truth is always within and when one questions often enough, then more and more brighter the truth and the light will shine, until eventually you do not need to search outwardly for light. For remember it is always here.

Jesus places his hand on his heart.

Question: Did you ever get to a point when you knew what you were here for?

Jesus: The answer to these words is: NOT SO. But what I had was a deep sense of trust and conviction within my Soul that was at most times unmovable. And I might also add the times when my trust, my convictions, became weakened, was not by my brothers or those who walked the planet as I; but from my own denial of

---

3. Jesus would not use the word religions, but instead chose to use "Houses".

my Father. When this occurred then I became separate from my Father and it was at this time that the temptations overpowered my being. Do you understand?

Questioners: Yes

Question: Master Jesus, people of the Christian faith talk about a "second coming".

Would it be the case that you would ever take human form again?

Jesus: There is much talk upon your planet of the "second coming". Man was once shown light, in this light he could also see his own light, this will never die. But man still fears his power and his light, so he hopes for a physical manifestation. The second coming is the acknowledgement of all ones light and power within their beings, it is their awakening. But this seems too simple a task, so many illusions are created.

Unfortunately, there has been little spiritual progress since, as a physical being, I walked this planet. Man still searches outwardly, when all is in here.

Jesus places his hand over his heart.

Question: Can you tell us actually how to look within?

Jesus gave this question some thought as he could have answered it quite a few times over. But, the answer he gave enabled an inner calmness to occur within the heart of each group member.....

Jesus: The most simple of keys to look inside one's Soul is the key of non-judgment; to keep an open outlook on everything. This is the most potent way to remember one's light.

Question: Why do you think man fears his light?

Jesus: It is not the light man fears as such, it is his own creative power. Man associates light with power, but there is a vast difference. Power is power, light is light. Many, many beings upon this planet have consciously chosen as yet not to own their own power. This is quite simply because they have yet to acknowledge their true light which shines, it shines upon all. For power can create good and power can create un-good. It is the same. If one is not specific in their purpose, they have not acknowledged their light and Creation within themselves, then the small degree of power they possess can be transmuted for un-light purposes. Many fear their power, not the light.

Question: How do we learn to use it to our best advantage?
Jesus: Your question is somewhat vague!

The questioner realizing the importance of being clear and precise rephrases the question...........

Question: What's the best way for us to use our power to become as we should be?
Jesus: Because many have chosen not to own their own power until they are light, they cannot use this. But there are many who wish power and yet light is not enough for them. To use your power for the highest, then first you must begin to integrate your power with your light; this is another task.

Question: How else may we acknowledge our light, or begin to do that?
Jesus: Quite simply remember all of you here and all your brothers and all your sisters and all peoples on this planet and all dimensions and beyond were created in light, in beauty and in joy. And all you have to do is simply remember this. Whenever you feel life beginning to burden you upon your shoulders replace the burden with a thought that is light. For example: a star......a rose......the wind and so on.

Your thoughts and your heart as one, perfectly balanced, will bring you light.

Question: Can you explain more about "Our Father"?

Jesus: The force that lives within each of you, within every cell of the Universes and beyond, is the force many know as the God-Force. It is this energy which holds all power both light and dark. For when mankind was created, he needed also the powers of dark to bring much solidness onto this planet. But dark is not essentially negative, there is a vast difference between negativity and darkness.

Negativity is not so much the opposite, more as the "in between", and it is these "in-between" and undirected forces that cause much disruption upon your planet.

But, it is so that ultimately the God-Force, the Creator of All, will have total power over this. But, in what way I cannot answer now. For to give a full answer to this question belittles the task many of you have chosen to do. Whether you feel this or not your self-worth will be lessened by having a direct answer. For it is by your own beings' searching and becoming the light that you are, that this negativity can diminish.

Question: Is there a central source of guidance or intelligence?

Jesus: There are, at the moment many sources, many stations where one goes to. To say where it begins and ends only limits Divine Creation. Every Divine particle in Creation contains intelligence of the Force. But; it is true to say that when one finds truth and surrender within, then one has accessed the central source of Creation.

The minds of many are somewhat limiting and so the comprehension within these minds is to limit also energy. There is no limit.

Question: Hello greetings. It sometimes seems very dark for mankind in the short term future. Are we going to learn to live with each other or are we bent on destruction?

Jesus: The outcome is always decided. The outcome is not decided by God, but by yourselves, I can share this much with you. The mere fact that many of you are beginning to feel the pain of others brings you to live with your brother.

There has been much written upon your planet of many impending disasters. Some of these words have been written from light, some from negativity. At this point I will say negativity creates much havoc, not dark. Do you all understand this?

no one responds, Jesus continues.......

I cannot tell you what will occur on your planet. But, I can tell you your hearts are more open now than they have ever been in all incarnations, by all peoples. But, when hearts begin to open illusions then begin to become, shall we say, dissipated. There becomes a struggle, for the illusions have had the ultimate control over mankind, but man's power and light begin to shine and the illusions crack.

This planet is to see many, many more false words enter into it. But remember always to open your heart and when-ever you feel fear, uncertainty, bleakness remember the most simplest of gifts that is ....a child. For there holds greatest beauty of all and by holding this image in your heart, you give no power to the illusions.

Question: Some people on this planet tend to look at Jesus and try to model themselves on the way they think you were. Do you think they are right to do this?

Jesus gives this question due consideration and after a long pause replies.....

Jesus: I choose not to acknowledge this.

Jesus gives the same response, a lack of acknowledgement to this question, as he did to a question in the previous meeting. Through his dismissal I could again experience why he does this. When he is asked to comment on a happening or a verbalization that he was supposedly to have said or done, he will not give it acknowledgment if the statement is false. For him to acknowledge an untruth only gives the untruth power.

If Jesus had responded by saying; "no that did not happen" or; "no I did not say that", he would be issuing a denial and so he would be acknowledging the power of the question. Every question has power, truthful or not, this is because we voice them or think of them. To stop an untruth from progressing further Jesus simply chooses not to acknowledge the question. Using an analogy, to play a game of tennis requires a minimum of two players, one serves the ball, the other hits it back (in this instance the ball is symbolic of the untruth). The ball will keep in play as long as it is being hit (acknowledged) by both players. As soon as one player stops hitting the ball it "dies". It has no more energy to bounce. Like wise, when an untruth is not acknowledged the energy of the untruth is no more.

Question: Master Jesus, I know one of your main tasks was to ground the Christ Energy onto the planet. What is the purpose of that?

Jesus: The purpose was bringing forth through my being, the Christ Power and Light. This occurred the moment that my being, my Soul, began to depart from this planet. I had no idea of this purpose at the time. There was much dark on your planet, much, much dark.

The energy of the Christ Power is a pure light energy that holds much transformation and much healing within its essence. This energy could only be grounded into your planet through a sacrifice. When this occurred, quite simply, the energy is born into each man, each woman, each child, each new Soul that enters this planet. For the planet then becomes enwrapped within this energy.

There are many, many energies that are light and many, many that are not so light, energies that can and cannot be brought into your planet through physical beings. Some energies can be brought through in the way we are tonight *(Through discernment and surrender to the flow of the Universe)*. There are also many beings who walk your planet who can take up the negative

33

energies which can then become transmuted by the light power.

The Christ Light and Power was brought in by our Father to save this planet and its peoples. The Christ Light and Power was not brought in to expel dark, but to bring much needed balance to this planet.

Question: Jesus, when people pray to Jesus do those prayers come to you or do they go to their own guides?
Jesus: When a child brings forth words that are searching, I do not hear these words.

Never is it words that I hear. For only when I am in a body like so *(indicating my bodily structure)* do I have the physical necessity to use such instruments as so *(gestures up to his ears)*.

It is always the heartfelt feelings that I feel. And so, in answer to your words, it is only when I feel these heartfelt feelings that I can respond.

Question: It seems from what you have explained, that a lot of your life was spent just following your inner trust and convictions. That consciously you knew very little at the time about your life's purpose. Is that true?
Jesus: If I was, as is written to be, a role model for mankind, then I also must perform as mankind. How could I possibly know outcome without first feeling pain? And so, in answer to your words, this is so *(Yes)*.

Question: How can different sects or religions kill each other in the name of God? I don't understand?
Jesus: There only is one light, one love and one Spirit. Many will use the words of light to create a self-created power. To have many different "houses" causes great separation and the main reason for such traumas within these "houses" is because one fears the other.

Light and dark are balanced by the greatest power of all, this is love. So do not try to understand what is going on, for your minds then become entangled also and you become part of these traumas.

Know always there is light, do not understand even the smallest of babes, but hold them within your heart. For understanding and reasoning comes from a mind that is confused. All this does is give more and more power to negative forces.

Question: Jesus can I ask you, if it is not a silly question, did you enjoy your life on Earth?

Jesus answered this question tenderly, each word precisely spoken and enhanced with profound compassion. Manifesting a unifying joy which filled his senses, as his memory grew in magnitude in remembrance of his physical life, Jesus responded....

Jesus: My life was the greatest gift my Father gave me.

The questioner probed deeper.........

Question: When other people have written about you it's always in such a serious way, I just wondered if you ever had any fun?

"Fun" was an innocently asked question. Jesus continues in joyous remembrance of the magic of life. Creation resonating through my body with an expanding sense of peace, Jesus asks.......

Jesus:

Do you listen to the wind?

Do you feel the stars shine upon your hair?

Do you taste the fresh waters?

Do you hold the tiniest of babes?

Do you rejoice in all Creation and feel the energy of light flowing into you?

Do you know peace within your Soul?

This for me was all.

Questioners: Thank you.

All the group members reported they were bathed in uplifting wonder as they heard and felt his joyful answer. For me, I humbled in being privy to experience such wonderful and un-conditional memories of Jesus. For the first time I could see and feel how great it is to be given life, which led me to a gratitude of my life.

Jesus: Now I shall depart, I will come to you all again.

Questioner: Thank you so much for coming to speak to us, it's been lovely. Do you have anything more to share with us?
Jesus: Only this, remember my essence as you will on this sacred occasion and remember how we talked as brothers...... Remember.

Questioners: Thank you.

4

The Unexpected

Four years had passed during which a number of channeling sessions had taken place; yet the Spirit of Jesus had not returned to communicate with us. Jesus had said he would once again return to speak about his life. Intuitively, I knew that such a moment had already been created by Universal timing and when that moment occurred he would come. My challenge, as always, was to be open enough to fit into that moment and to be able to feel this Universal timing, along with the presence of Jesus, or whichever Spirit or Energy was around and waiting to communicate and share any relevant information.

During these years I had moved with the family to the South of England. After settling my children into their new environment, I gave birth to my fourth child - a little girl. In between being a mum and partner, the Universe would guide me to when a Spirit or Energy would like to communicate. Around three hundred new Energies connected with my psyche, along with a few familiar ones. They communicated new understandings as to the workings of the Universe and Creation. These communications were very profound and contained Universal lessons and insights which continually expanded my understanding of God / Creation and empowered my way of living.

People often ask me if I feel exhausted by the seemingly vast amount of Spiritual connections and the intensity of the information that I receive. The effects of these spiritual meetings were quite the opposite; leaving me feeling incredibly clear in both mind and Spirit – sparkling with renewed vigor.

Fuelled by the understandings that were shared, along with the purity of energy these Spirits and Energies emanated; it was with great ease that I was able to switch from my everyday family duties to receiving Spirit communications.

The on-going Spiritual Expansion within my psyche introduced me to an innate ability where upon my consciousness would literally travel back in time. This phenomena occurred a few days before the third Christmas in our now not so new home.[4]

Time Travel to Observe the Birth of Jesus

With Christmas just around the corner, I had decided to give myself the extra chore of cleaning the house from top to bottom! Whilst stripping off the settee covers in preparation of a "good old scrubbing", I spontaneously felt what could only be described as a doorway ethereally beginning to "open". My entire being was filled with a great surge of excitement and energy. It was a eureka moment, as I suddenly became aware that an opportunity had become available to travel back in time to observe the birth of Jesus. Wow! This was a completely spontaneous and unexpected insight, something I would have never consciously thought of or would have ever imagined to be possible.

For the next few hours I kept my eureka moment quiet. I wanted to be absolutely certain of what I was sensing. The concept of Time Travel was completely new to me and on immediate logical consideration unfathomable. I didn't say anything about it to Adrian. He would have been extremely excited about this possibility. He constantly encourages me when my psyche is presented with new spiritual "doorways", perhaps not opened before by mans' consciousness. His enthusiasm would have added pressure for me to respond to this insight. Pressure is to be avoided at all costs, otherwise clarity in ones psyche becomes difficult (clarity that is to discern if and when the time is Universally correct to step through a new doorway of understanding).

4. For additional Time Travel information see 'Journey Home'.

By early evening, and with the feeling to Time Travel through this unknown "doorway" growing stronger and stronger, I decided to tell Adrian what was happening. As predicted he was very excited indeed! The feeling within me had now become so strong that I was not influenced in any way by Adrian's excitement.

From long experience, I know that I am at my best and most comfortable doing my spiritual activities in a tidy house. So, unless the house is tidy I do not do any spiritual work. With four children the house is normally in a fairly messy state! Unfortunately, I was "buzzing" with so much energy - caused by this imminent Time-Travelling experience - that I couldn't concentrate on housework at all. Fortunately, fuelled by his excitement, Adrian had the place spotless in no time. My focus was kept on the "doorway" in time, which seemed to be growing larger and larger. My children are usually late to bed which would not have been conducive to any major spiritual journeying (since I would have been too physically tired to focus). To my surprise the children had taken themselves off to bed by 8.00pm and my youngest had fallen asleep by 7.30pm. The opportunity had been created with ease. Adrian and I sat quietly in our front lounge. I closed my eyes and begun settling into my process of surrender....

The Journey Begins

As my head was gently eased back, my will stepped aside and a strong and loving energy entered and introduced herself as the Great Mother Energy. This was an energy that encompassed every aspect of motherhood - not just for mankind, but for every-thing; the birds, the animals, the sea creatures, plants, flowers, trees, etc. She seems to be the mother of all things in this dimension. The Great Mother Energy said to us *(Adrian was to travel back also)* "You must let go of all that you have learned of this most sacred of nights."

This in itself was quite a challenge. Having grown up in a predominantly Christian country, we had of course been subjected to vast amounts of "information" since our earliest childhood days regarding Jesus' birth. In fact, as I'm sure is the case for so many people in the western world, the first play we had both ever acted in was the nativity at infant school. And because this is such an impressionable age, those scenes from the play were ingrained in our memories. So, "to let go" - yes that was going to be tough!

The Great Mother then began guiding us, through a series of breaths, to loosen our consciousness and travel through the wormhole. The process took around five minutes, during which breaths were held and released in various ways (each time encouraged by her to go "back, back, back"), until at last our energy slowed and then stopped. [5]

"Now be aware - what is it you see?" she asked.

Bringing my awareness into focus, I was convinced I had travelled to the wrong destination. It wasn't as I was expecting it to be. In front of me was a stone cobbled track, while to my right side were a number of small single-storey white buildings. The one I was standing next to had a small window and a wooden door. It was early evening, night was just falling. My initial response to this scene was confusion with regard to the cobbled path; in my mind I had expected some sort of dirt track. Sensing my confusion, The Great Mother reminded me, "Let go of any expectations." Calmed by these words we took another deep breath and moved slightly forward in time to the evening.

We remained in the same area as before, but now I saw in front of me a tall man and a very weary lady who was quite small - around 5 ft 2" to 5ft. 3" in height. Instantly, I knew this was Mary and Joseph. As I looked at Mary and Joseph I wondered; "Where's the donkey?" And even more confusingly, Mary was holding a

---

5. Wormhole – a scientifically established phenomena. A vortex-like connection between now and some moment in the past.

young child? (A boy who looked to be around the age of two and half years old). Intuitively, I knew this was Mary's son! But, this didn't make any sense at all. Again I wondered whether I had "got off at the wrong stop"? The Great Mother reassured us once again: "Let go of everything you have ever learned of this night - you must let go." This was even tougher than I thought it was going to be! There was no donkey and Mary already had a son. I had to let go of everything that I had been taught at school about Jesus' birth... The Great Mother drew a breath into me and I started to relax and open my mind fully to the travelling experience.

Joseph and Mary entered the small white building next to me. Inside was a seat near the door and Mary, looking very relieved, sat down with her young boy in her arms. Could this building be the Inn that is traditionally spoken about? It was certainly packed with people.

Joseph walked over to the right hand corner of the Inn (*I don't actually know whether it was an Inn, but for simplicity's sake I shall refer to it as such*). He spoke to a man who was standing behind a dark-colored wooden bar, and appeared to be in charge of the place.

There were some rooms through a couple of doorways, sealed by curtains, that also had a number of people in them. But I could sense that these rooms were occupied by local people. The man shook his head - whatever Joseph had requested, it was not forth-coming. However, as he walked back towards Mary he was joined by an elderly woman who, seeing Mary was exhausted, took the child from her and asked them to follow her. They went out of the Inn, turning right up the cobbled path. I was aware of two or three dwellings opposite the Inn and buildings to either side - these houses were detached from each other and appeared to be private homes. After passing a couple of buildings close by to the Inn, the old lady (*who looked to be around 60 or so years old*) turned right into what appeared to be the town square. We entered the courtyard, which had buildings on each of its four sides. On the left she indicated the town barn - they could rest there. We went in through two large doors and the barn was filled from top to bottom with hay. There was only hay, I couldn't see any animals.

My body breathed in again, following the instructions of the Great Mother Energy, causing us once again to move slightly forward in time. It was now very late at night - whether it was the same day, I am not sure. Mary, Joseph and the old lady were inside the barn, the lady had the boy-child in her arms. Suddenly there was a lot of commotion, running footsteps and a sense of general panic occurring outside. Three men then ran into the barn and snatched the child from the old lady, who appeared panic stricken. It was a very frightening scene.

The men, dressed in everyday clothing, ran out with the child. Soon after, they came back into the barn. It appeared that they were looking for more young children. Joseph stood in front of his very pregnant wife. Up until now, others had not been able to detect Mary's pregnancy as she had worn long loose fitting robes and had carried a small child into town. Joseph was shaking his head in determination, as the men were asking and looking for more children.

Mary was very frightened indeed. I knew the child they had snatched *(Mary's son)*, was to be killed. This whole scene happened so fast and was unexpected in what was otherwise a very peaceful time. It was a time to rest, especially for Mary.

What was interesting for me at the time was how my emotions were somehow being kept under control. For this scene to be fully appreciated, it needed to be observed with absolute dispassion. However, as a mother of four I am very passionate about children and would normally be desperately disturbed by any scenes of children being hurt, abused or unloved. So, I couldn't understand how my emotions were being kept from me. It was a very surreal situation.

My body breathed in and we moved slightly forward in time.

Mary was giving birth behind a red curtain that had been erected in the barn. Whether this was the same night or one that followed, I am uncertain. The curtain I felt was symbolic so that privacy could be given to the birth - even though I was observing purely in energy form *(the same form as the Spirits who watch and help us are adopting)*, it is decreed by Universal Law that some things are kept private. A young lady, in her mid 20s from the Inn, was assisting in the birth. The old lady was not visible in this scene.

We then moved forward slightly to the hours before dawn. I guessed that we were about to see the baby, and I wondered whether he would have the halo with which he is usually depicted in pictures. I always felt it was rather fanciful, but I suppose it demonstrated his uniqueness. *(I say unique rather than special, as of course all babies are very special!)*

My time then came to look at this babe. My energy gazed down in awe as I looked at him. Oh! This was indeed a beautiful, beautiful, child; so clear and vibrant, he was physically strong and obviously very healthy. Indeed, I was surprised by his size - for some reason I had expected him to be smaller. As I looked into his blue eyes, everything around me seemed silent. I marveled in the pureness and freedom he exuded. And to my astonishment the child did indeed have, emanating from his shoulders and over his head, a haze of white light filled with what appeared to be hundreds of stars; some bigger, some smaller, all shining away. The child appeared focused in his energy and seemed oblivious to the traumatic events which had recently occurred.

Mesmerized, I did not want to leave the purity and safeness of his presence. But slowly my energy drew away from him and I observed the wider scene. I cannot say if he was in a manger or not, although whatever he lay in was fairly small, filled with hay and then covered with cloth.

Three children then entered the barn through a small door on the right. These children, two boys and one girl, were aged between six to eight years. I was initially confused as to why they had not also been taken and killed, since I had sensed that the men who had taken Mary's child from the arms of the old lady had a desire to kill all small children. However, I then realized that these children weren't so small and their older ages had saved them.

I did not see any shepherds and I was not aware of any great star. However, in the next scene I did encounter the wise men. I was shown telepathically that two had travelled from the East together and one travelled from the Southeast.

"Do you see what they wear on their heads?" the Great Mother asked.

Each of them wore differently styled headdresses measuring about 18" in height. The Great Mother, with awe, reverence and honor towards the "wise ones" (this is how she referred to them), said slowly and deeply; "These wise ones are so wise, so great is their wisdom, that their heads must always be higher than anyone else (hence the headdress). They are revered more than kings."

Her energy swelled in my heart when she said this, I could feel the enormity of their wisdom.

The next breath took me to the moment when the wise ones arrived at the barn where the babe lay. For me, this was the best part of my experience, and I could really sense their energy 100%, since I had no physical body to restrict my feelings.

The Great Mother gently said; "So honored are the wise ones they bow to no one, but, do you see, in the presence of this child, they cannot bow low enough."

My whole being felt it would burst from the great and pure joy they exuded as they bowed low before the babe. In this moment, I realized that - although in my present life I have experienced happiness, peace and some joy - never had I experienced anything like this joy that these wise ones exuded; a joy that felt so pure, on such a high scale. It was the most wonderful and empowering feeling imaginable. I soaked it in for a few moments. Later one of the wise ones lit some incense and began to smoke it around the babe. "This is to cleanse the child's aura, as the child was born in traumatic circumstances," the Great Mother told us.

I looked at the child and at his energy and thought how clear both were; the child's head and neck still surrounded by hundreds of stars. If only they could see what I see, they would know he was just fine. Another of the wise ones mixed some substance into a small bowl of water and began to bathe the child's feet.

Suddenly I felt the window beginning to close.

"We have to go back," the Great Mother said; "Take a deep breath and I will guide you back."

Following her instructions we returned to this present time. As I opened my eyes, a great sadness fell over me, which felt almost like homesickness. I was left with no doubt that my physical body had undergone a deep shift in perspective as a result of the Time-Travel experience and the energies that I had encountered. Silence to the experience rang through me, physically, mentally, emotionally and spiritually. I needed time to absorb every thing that I had seen and felt along with experiencing Time-Travel. Without a doubt I knew this ability to access history as it happens was an ability that all humankind would one day have access to; resulting in the end of wars and conflicts that are caused by mass confusion.

Using an analogy; the experience "found" the missing pieces to the jigsaw puzzle of Jesus' birth, whilst removing the pieces that had been forced into the jigsaw - but didn't ever really fit. A clear picture emerged, a picture filled with sense and understanding as to who this man truly was.

The Universal Flow had revealed this ability to Time-Travel to me over a period of years, as I continued *(through tough personal experiences and situations)* to free my psyche from the written words of history, resulting in a continued expansion of my consciousness - opening to possibilities that I could not have before comprehended.

Another four years passed, with as much work and family

duties as the previous four, alongside the continued Universally inspired channeled sessions.

Adrian worked as a Chiropractor in our very busy clinic. He met all sorts of people who required his services. He would share details of the channeled sessions to a number of patients who were receptive and could comprehend this "spiritual technique" of channeling. Interest in the spiritual abilities I was presented with grew rapidly. It was the beginning of the always now asked question; "why do you think you were chosen to do this work?"

People would make their own individual conclusions to their questioning. From my perspective, I simply do what my body / psyche was created to do.

Great advice was once given to me by a very wise lady; "you are only responsible for delivering the absolute truth from what you experience, you are not responsible as to whether someone gets it or not." Hearing the richness and simplicity of those words strengthened my internal responsibility and path in life, whilst respecting *(though not always understanding)* the paths of everyone I meet. Without knowing why at times certain individuals come together, individuals who would not usually in their every day life situations connect. Somehow a momentary "spark" of expansion is created to attract these people together for a short but fruitful time.

It was one of these unprecedented connections of paths that brought the next group of people into my life, their collective Spirit igniting the third channeled meeting with Jesus.

Nine people arrived to my home for what was to be a very interesting session along with a surprise meeting. Clearing myself as always, I began my surrender....

The first Spirit to connect was very anxious indeed, this Spirit was surrounded in a fog of nervousness. Mentally I tried to reassure this Spirit, but the nervousness that enveloped this Spirit confused the group as to when to voice their "welcome". The connection the Spirit had made to my body was strong, yet its'

essence seemed without confidence to speak. I had not experienced this difficulty in a Spirit before.

I knew that the Spirit would leave my body unless someone
quickly communicated. Finally, Adrian sensing the Spirits
struggle gave a warm and encouraging acknowledgement.
Adrian reassured the Spirit that it was safe to speak.

Drawing upon all the courage held within its' essence the
Spirit bowed low to the group, slowly rising my head to
speak.......

5

Peter

"The truth was not enough and
so I began to - shall we say -
expand on the truth."

Peter: I am known to all as the one that is known as Peter.

Questioners: Welcome.

Peter: Now I come for truth. My task now is one of utmost importance. For many times throughout these cycles of the planet
untruths have been spoken. I come now with......

*A long period of silence now occurs, Peter is finding it emotionally
difficult to speak and to continue with the task which brought him to
speak to us all.*

The child I talk through gives to me strength. I ask now for
strength from you all. The task I have on this evening is for me
so.....

*Another long period of silence, Peter is troubled and appears to be
uncomfortable with himself. One of the people present senses Peter's
hurt and distress.*

Questioner: Dear Peter you are most welcome here, do not feel
afraid.

*With this reassurance, Peter finds the confidence in himself to
emotionally step forward to speak.*

Peter: Now I can talk and with much direction I shall, on this most
sacred of nights, aim to put right that which was not so. Many

words have been written in books and many of these words came forth from my being. Now you can see why this is so hard. Yes, it is so that I walked for many cycles with the being whom you all know as Jesus. We walked as brothers, such was the trust from my Master. So much that my ego grew strong.

Many people came to me upon his departure from this planet. And at first it was true that it was my intention to share all that had been spoken between us all. But yet these words were simple and no judgment is placed now, but from my being I sensed, and now I know this sense was from my ego, that many peoples wanted more.

The truth was not enough and so I began to, shall we say, expand on the truth. For many cycles I have felt so alone. And now I give you my true light and ask that you all see how easily stories can be mis-told.

Some members of the group asked for confirmation to the full identity of the residing Spirit….

Question: Are you Peter the disciple?
Peter: How the word begins to make my Soul heavy. For when I walked with Jesus so, so ,so, always so we walked as brothers. Never once did he refer to my being as "his disciple". And yet I glorified in the response from many with that description. And so I ask now for your kindness and your light, to remember me as a brother to my brother.

Question: We surely do. May I ask you, was your truth buried beneath man's greed's and dogmas?
Peter: My truth went out the moment Jesus departed and that truth as yet has never been brought forth. It was not because of my fellow man that I became so. But of my own.

Question: Could you share the truths with us this evening?
Pausing at this question, Peter answers…..

Peter: You are waiting for my very, very, very, very, dear one.

Feeling the pain in Peters' Spirit, it was clear to me that he was not here to elaborate on Jesus' life, but to elucidate his part in the enhancement of the stories of Jesus. He wanted to lay claim to his exaggerations that have resulted in a deviation from the truth of his dear friends life. Peter took responsibility for a lot of the confusion which is held within some religions; confusions resulting in blockages within the minds of man. This has created a consequential restriction in Universal Flow which in turn prevents the spiritual growth of mankind. Such was the burden of remorse from Peter.

Everyone at this gathering, through Peters' pain, recalled that we had all exaggerated at some time or another. The group humbled in his remorse and silently began to realize the power of the spoken word and to speak in truth or not at all.

Peters' visit was a great lesson, with his honesty uniting us all.

Questioner: Peter can I say something. I pray very much that if you feel any pain or any heaviness that now you may let that go. And that I am sure within my heart that we understand and thank you for coming today.

Questioner: And for sharing that very human emotion and I think we can all relate to that. I too give you my love and my light and hope that heaviness may go to.

The following was asked as the pain was so great that Peter carried. The questioner asked this so that Peters' Spirit would be energized with a sense of lightness. It was a good question, in as much as it not only had the desired results, but it gave remembrance the power of an uplifting thought.

Question: Could you share just one thing with us. I understand what you have said, but can you share perhaps a fun time you had with Jesus. I know you probably had many?

Peter thought awhile and his Spirit began to lift with warm remembrance.

Peter: The time that springs most from my heart was the time each one of us held within our hands stones. And the aim of the stones was to create many jumps.

Peter gestures with his hand the stone jumping on the water's surface.

It was so that I was the one who created the most. Maybe this is why I hold the memory so.

Finally, Peters' Spirit was filled with an inequitable joy as he remembered a time of skimming the pebbles with four friends, one of whom was Jesus. They, standing at the waters edge of a large calm lake, where an abundant collection of alternative stones (warmed by the sun) lay on the sand and tall grasses standing motionless alongside gave a sense of stillness in the heat of the day. Friendly banter marking the occasion of the competition, which already had an expected outcome. Peter being highly skilled in this pastime of skimming the pebbles was as yet unbeaten! And it seems he remained unbeaten! He was rather pleased at this. Peter's Spirit bowed to the group as he departed with a sense of freedom and lightness embracing his Spirit.

My head was eased back to allow Peter's Spirit to disengage itself as my body then took a deep breath to draw safely the next Spirit to use form. In fondness and familiarity the Spirit bowed low and touched my heart in acknowledgement of the group and the evenings session. The Spirit spoke......

6

The Missing Years

"You Have All the Answers,
You Have Read Many Books,
And Yet How Many Beings Have Read Themselves?"

Jesus: I am known to all as the Master Jesus. Now we can all share this most joyous of evenings with also my friend (*referring to Peter, who was observing close by, and had chosen to stay for the evening*).

For so, so long he has hidden. Now he walks. You may ask.......

Bowing again and opening his right hand to indicate he was ready to receive the evenings questions....

Question: Can you tell us about your immaculate conception?
Jesus: The conception or as you place the words "immaculate" was not quite so. My mother whom you all know as the Virgin Mary was indeed of supreme grace. But so much has been miswritten. It is as it was, when I first came to this planet through the energy of a new born babe, that indeed within my family there was also another child. This child was my blood brother. But this is not spoken of. My blood brother was conceived between my mother and my father.

Questioner: Thank you.

Question: I would so like to ask another question. As you were such a tremendous philosopher whose truths were so profound. If your truth had been told by the church as you gave it to the world, would we now have reached the "Golden Age"?

Jesus: My simple words, I taught and I shared many feelings of life and beyond within groups like so. It was not for my being to conform to any formal structure as you speak. When you have structures *(organized belief systems and ways of living)* you have limitations and you have power.

And so for my words to enter such domains was not so. My words were free and your own Golden Age is there ready if only you listen to your heart.

Question: Jesus when you were a child did you feel different to other children?
Jesus: My childhood was spent in awe of all Creation. You asked did I feel so different. The answer to your question is, a child only feels truth. And in that truth I could see also the truth in others. At times I would be somewhat unruly and somewhat abrasive. I would sometimes instigate games which in my being I felt was fun and yet would offend others. But always I felt as one with all children.

Question: How did the insights come to you and when did you begin to talk with people, when did that begin?
Jesus: For many, many cycles my greatest pleasures came from being with other People, discovering different paths and under-standings.

You asked if I have or had insights. But my whole life was an insight. All words were spoken with glory.

Question: There is very little known about what happened to you when you became between the ages of 12 and 13 years of age? Where did you go?
Jesus: Now are you asking did I travel, did I move home, was I schooled. Which is your question?

Question: It is said that you travelled and came to England with your uncle.

Jesus: My Uncle was indeed a merchant. And it was not unlikely for many young children to travel like so. I would travel to many different continents. Most of my life of which you speak was spent travelling. And most was selling goods.

Question: Is it true as we have been told that you used to go to many schools of learning such as the Tibetan Llamas?

Jesus: My schools would often be places where indeed structures would be built *(churches, temples)* as you have spoken of. And, I would go not so much to learn but more to understand others' wisdoms.

For me to understand the wisdom of others was a great learning for my own wisdom. And so, I can say that it was not their wisdom that I took, but my own wisdom that came forth.

Question: Was it a sorrow to you that your own people never understood or recognized your wisdom?

Jesus: Are you referring now to my later times?

Question: To the Jews.

Jesus: My sorrow was only because many had to ask and could not see for themselves. And yet when things were shown still many could not see.

Questioner: Thank you.

Question: Can I ask a question? There's an ancient tradition that you received early training with the Essene brotherhood, is this so?

Jesus: Now I feel you refer to the times of around my 18th cycle *(18 Years)*. Is this so? During times of my later young manhood, I became rather of one mind shall we say. And yes I went to join many that I felt could answer my confusion.

The times before my 18th cycle for me were of much physical growth. But, in some ways this growth into manhood kept me from my own wisdom. And quite simply I felt that these beings, whom you talk of, could give me the joy that I was searching for.

I realized by the time of around my 28th cycle that this was not so. For often elements of holding back would occur in those teachings. And yet also from the age of 18 and onwards, in my heart there was not the strength to move on with conviction. I was confused and so I searched.

Question: May I ask a question on behalf of the child that you talk through? She would like to know if you physically fathered a child?

I had asked for one of the group to ask this question as there had been numerous stories past and present that Jesus had children. I had hoped at the previous sessions with Jesus that the question would be asked.

Jesus: The answer to your question is so (yes). On more than one occasion. And these moments of birth brought forth much strength in my heart.

Question: Can I ask how many?

Jesus slowly counts how many on the left hand using the right index finger, as he fondly remembers his children.

Jesus: Four, one a son and three daughters.

As Jesus recalls these memories I felt the children to have been born during his teen years. And they were not from the same woman. I could feel through his memory there had been three fruitful relationships, two were strong and the third quite brief.

Question: So you have a bloodline?

Jesus: I have a bloodline, but it is the line that I embarked on before I began to feel the conviction within my essence *(when he was a teenager)*. My bloodline is a line that is written. But you will not find it until fear no more governs the "houses" of belief systems.[6]

Many choose to exaggerate stories, many say I lived *(after the crucifixion)* but my body was not immortal. It was no more immune to pain and suffering as yours are.

Question: You said that at the age of 28 you (for want of a better word) stepped forward with your conviction. Is this when people began to come and listen to you, as is written?
Jesus: Many would come when I was a young boy, because I was unclouded. It was not so much the words I spoke, but my clarity, my inner strength. And yes when I became around 28 cycles, once more I regained that strength. The people were always there, but I was not ready.

Question: Was it really necessary for you to die on the cross or was it man that sent you to the cross?
Jesus: My task ultimately on this planet was to end this way. So often man has been blamed for my death and yet you need to remember that this planet was so confused. So much dark was upon this Earth plane. My task was to become a sacrifice. I could have walked away. And yet deep within my Soul I knew that my task was to end.

Question: Are you saying then Jesus that when you walked the Earth you were not bound by Karmic law?
Jesus: By "Karmic law" I feel you mean what you do, so comes back. Is this not so?
Questioner: Yes.

Jesus: But there is still this confusion as to "Karmic law" on your planet. Often Karma stems from an ego point. When I left the

---

6. I felt there physically exists a written documentation of Jesus' bloodline which has not yet been revealed or perhaps even discovered.

planet, one could assume the crucifixion would create Karma. Is that not so?

Questioner: Yes.

Jesus: Yet it was all perfect. No Karma was created. No Karma. Karma is a subject that will need more discussion. But not from my being.[7]

Question: Could I ask something about the healings that occurred. I know that you have already explained that many healings did occur. What does it take for somebody to be healed or for somebody to become physically well again?

Jesus: What it takes is quite simply for the child to feel his light.

Having previously detailed as to how and why the healings occurred, Jesus' answer was short. There was an expectancy from everyone that a more detailed answer would be given. Jesus felt the simplicity of the answer had been missed by the group. Sensing this Jesus continues.....

Jesus: And yet the answer is simple, but you all want more?
With this reverse questioning, the group, feeling somewhat embarrassed at missing Jesus' simple but potent answer accepted they had waited for a more elaborate reply as they smiled and appreciated the simplicity of the answer.

Question: Can I ask about when you were 28 and when you traveled? Why did you feel that to continue your task and to finish it that you went back to Israel, your place of birth. Why could you not complete your task in one of the other countries that you had visited?

Jesus: Shall we quite simply say, there was home.

---

7. See chapter 10 on Karma.

Question: Could I ask you a very practical question? In our physical world there is much focus placed on money and people become very stressful because they do not have money or that they need more money. Did you ever have problems with money and working with money?

Jesus: I hear your words...... but I sense your feelings and your words do not match your feelings?

The questioner admitted to having a hang up about "not having enough money and needing more to attain a personal sense of peace".

We had not such a control as you have in these years. More in the time when I walked on the planet honor was greater than the coins.

Words were honor and often deeds or work or however you wish to call your daily task were rewarded by the efforts of others. Coins were not so vast.

Question: Jesus, you were known as a Messiah and the occidental religions talk of the second coming of the Messiah. Will this happen?

Jesus: This confusing statement is always asked. (*Having addressed the Messiah questions in previous channeled sessions*) And I say as I always say; I walked the planet as man, as my brother no greater, no lesser. I walked as man. I died as man.

At the point of my death the Christ Energy became inherent in all beings. No more shall I come in physical form to this planet.

Jesus' Spirit becomes quiet as he observes most questions asked are from what one has read or externally been taught. His energy focuses intently scanning all the members of the group and then inquiringly asks....

Jesus: You Have All the Answers. You Have Read Many Books and Yet How Many Beings Have Read Themselves?

Pensively the group thank Jesus for these centralizing words.

Question: The purpose of you coming as the "son of God". Christians believe it was for the forgiveness of sin. Was it so, or is this something much greater than this beyond the world which we can understand. Was it for example, divine love?

Jesus: My arrival upon this planet was of joy and of light. So much had I grown to enjoy the fruits of the Mother Earth. There is so much written from different "houses" as to why I came here in the first place.

Does one truly need a reason to be given such an incredible gift as life. Sin is only in the minds of man, it does not exist within the heart and Soul of the Universe, of our Father, of the Creator. Sin is a by-product of man's ego. It is not something our Father chooses to acknowledge. And so therefore that may be an answer to your question.

But my *(Soul)* task was indeed to depart from this planet upon the cross, with the pain of man deep within my Soul.

Question: Can I ask about the Christ Energy? You explained before that the second coming would be an acknowledgement within us of the Christ Energy. How then may we begin to work to that acknowledgement or feel that in our being?

Jesus: Always remember you were created in light. And in that light only simplicity survives.

To acknowledge the Christ Light or the Christ Energy within your Soul is to remember that you are only here in the body for a short, short time. And that your Spirit exists and is far greater than you can possibly imagine. Do not limit your feelings to that just of body.

Question: Tell me Jesus, we have been given to understand that you said; "My Father's house had many mansions". Could you enlarge upon that?

Jesus: My father's house so, so, so, *(Jesus gestures with his hands the vastness of our Father).*

59

The words that I spoke were quite simply that my Father's heart holds many, many rooms. And this was symbolic.

Question: So really the church did not enlighten us on the symbology of this?
Jesus: If you looked only inside yourself you would not have required such a structure *(formal place of worship)* to answer for you.

Many may feel now my words do not answer fully what they ask. But it is already inside you. It is for your beings to begin to break down all the ideals you have placed and raised within so many churches and so many different houses of beliefs. It is not for my being to do that for you. For only you built them and only you can bring them down. And so if my words seem somewhat vague then it is quite simply I choose not to break down what you have built.

Questioner: Thank you.
Jesus: Now I shall say one more question.

Question: Dare I ask a question about Judas Iscariot?
Jesus' Spirit silences; the cells in my body withdraw as Jesus enters a darkness of injustice, born out of mankind's projected false understanding of Judas. Jesus deepens into this consuming darkness, before his heart becomes flooded with timeless love, honor and deep, deep gratitude for Judas. He speaks firmly – his words denouncing the spiritual imprisonment of Judas.....
Jesus: Much has been written and much has been miswritten. He was and is my friend.

Jesus understood the sincerity of Judas' path, he understood how Judas created the opening for the completion and ease of his task (which was to ground a pure energy into the earth) and in doing so reverberate into the hearts of mankind. Jesus knew the unconditional love and "bravery" that was his friend Judas.

Question: Thank you for that, for I believe that he was the only one capable of receiving "Sin" without his Soul being damaged. Is that so?

Jesus: And now I feel a strength inside to say quite firmly, his task seemingly was with as you all put it "in sin" and yet if his task was not completed then the Christ Light would not be alive on your planet.

Now I feel I must depart, but only because my friend waits here. *(Peter's Spirit continued to wait for Jesus to finish the session, but I do not have any idea as to where they went after the session had ended.)*

And also your last question for my being was most potent.

I clearly felt Jesus wanted the session to end with understanding the unconditional sacrifice made by Judas to assist Jesus in his task.

Questioners: Thank you Jesus for coming. I hope one day you will come again.

Jesus: Many times I shall come.

Questioners: Thank you.

This session made me realize how much of Jesus' life has been denied and falsely reported. I could not understand why this should be? Surely no one who knew and loved him for himself could have possibly recorded so many untruths?

With each session Jesus' Spirit grew in strength and clarity as his life on Earth was understood.

The following years saw my ability to Time-Travel progress. It was this process of Time-Travel that the Universal Flow expanded within me - I guess so that I could understand and accept this intrinsic aspect of mankind's collective persona. Seven years passed before Jesus' Spirit returned, and so with Universal timing I planned another session. At this session a diverse number of people were invited, this to generate a broader selection of questions that stem from the individuals under-standing of Jesus.

The previous year had seen a huge amount of public interest in Jesus' companion, *Mary Magdalene. I felt it was this interest that drew Jesus' Spirit near, and in so doing inspire the planning of another evening session.*

My preparation, as for all channeling sessions, included decorating the meeting room with an abundance of flowers, candles, and incense, as I consciously worked at clearing my mental and emotional levels - before finally preparing myself physically for the evening ahead.

About thirty minutes or so before I begin a session I am filled with total peace and serenity. When this occurs I feel the Spirit/s who are to grace our evenings session come close to me, so much so that I am not comfortable in exchanges of small talk to anyone - my focus is now on the task ahead.

Minutes before my total surrender to the Universe the invited group enter the prepared and spiritually energized room. I make sure they are all comfortable with their seats, as smiles and reassurances are shared, before I settle into my process of connection.

Three minutes later the first Spirit, filled with feminine grace, enters my body and introduces herself..........

7

Mary Magdalene

"My path was lost
but through the words that were spoken to my heart
I became found..."

Mary: I am the energy of the one who is now in many people's minds on this planet. My name when I walked upon the soils of many lands was known to all as Mary of Magdalene. I come because there is much speculation of my existence, and so I come to answer what you may wish to ask.

Mary placed the preposition "of" before Magdalene, giving an understanding that in those times the individual's last name was that of the "house"; the collective family members were known. The identity of the "house" being the predominating feature of identity and roots.

Question: When did you first meet the person known as Jesus?
Mary: My life before I came into great wonder of such a true being of God was somewhat of a slight dark. My path was lost but through the words that were spoken to my heart I became found. I washed all my old way of living and I became the consort of the man you all hold in great wonder, as is now as was then *(indicating Jesus was revered by the people then, as he is by many now).*

Question: Did you actually marry Jesus? *(Asking the question with slight assumption that Mary was indeed referring to Jesus in her answer to the previous question).*
Mary: My life did not dictate that I could marry. I was cast aside from all who felt I was unclean and so it was not permitted for us to marry as such. But *(said in joy)* for a very short while our lives

63

became as one.

Question: And did you conceive children from Jesus?
Mary: My life with the most wonderful man in all of creation could not be blessed with children. I became barren because in my youth I was in a very dark time where there was much abuse. (*I felt this abuse to be physical, maybe some type of attack which had left Mary damaged internally*) And so to have born a child was not within my destiny.

Question: How long did you stay together?
Mary: We joined for two full cycles (*years*) and it was before my great love passed. (*died*). Now I shall depart.
Questioners: Thank you.

Mary now leaves my body and with a great rush filled with familiarity the next Spirit enters. Acknowledging the group, the spirit begins the communication......

8

The Third Meeting

"One cannot be taught,
one can only expand,
as one lets go of all their restricting thought forms.
Each individual is their greatest teacher.
And yet we look to others to guide us."

Jesus: I am the one you know as the Master Jesus.
Questioners: Welcome.

Jesus: I come and I am in great joy to be here once more. I come in light and in great wonderment at all your Spirits who have gathered here to share words with my essence. And so I say I am here in joy!

Questioner: Thank you, thank you for coming to talk to us. May I ask the first question?

Question: Were you ever told about the Wise Men who came to see you just after you were born?
Jesus: When I grew as a small boy there was much disharmony. My father was pained and my mother cast aside, so there was not much that could be told of my birth.

Two years after Time-Travelling to watch Jesus' birth. Mary's Spirit showed herself to me on a number of occasions instilling a request for me to travel back in time to her life, so that she could relive the truth of her life. Her Spirit had weakened in the lack of acknowledgement to the truth of her life. This astoundingly heart wrenching account is published in 'Journey Home'.

Question: What of Joseph your father, how old was he when he died?
Jesus: My father became an ally for much learning within the new way of understanding what you call religion. He lived many years and he died a wise man. There was much he could not understand, but there was much he was willing to learn. And his life ended long, long, long, long, long, long, long.......
My understanding from Jesus' response was that Joseph died after Jesus, and therefore Jesus was not able to give a direct answer to the length of Joseph's life.

Question: Did your father Joseph understand who you were?
Jesus: My father was greatly respected. But my mother was cast aside, and so it was difficult for him to acknowledge my life as his son. And so I cannot answer this question.

Question: Who did you grow up with if your mother was cast aside?
Jesus: My childhood was free and my childhood was joyful, I played with the children of my mother's sister. We played and we grew as a family so I have much connection to my good, good, good friends. When I became more with questions, I travelled with my great uncle and I visited many lands and many seas.

In these lands I learnt much of other cultures. I began also to learn of many histories.

This was a great time in my life and it was the time I felt most free! To learn of others ways is quite an honor!

"Great uncle" was not a term of age that Jesus had used to describe him, but of respect and trust that he had for this wonderful man who showed him the world!

Question: Did you learn how to read and write?
Jesus: The written word was not for me. My ability to stay and study was not so great, but through tongue I learnt languages and

this was for my life was far greater.

Question: Were you aware of the Old Testament...the Hebrew Testament, the prophecy, that a new King of Israel would come?
Jesus: Many (*people*) of my life were taught always of the old way of living and belief. And it was a form of understanding that we were all expected to adhere to. But I found that I would question these old ways. They seemed too neat! They did not leave room for one to think or question. The ability of thinking and questioning was taken away as a right and this did not sit comfortably with my essence.

You talk of a prophecy of a great King coming, well we all had to have hope so this was always shared, this prophecy.

This prophecy kept us in line, if you like, but it did not sit comfortably within my essence.

Question: As you became older, into adulthood, did others think that you were the person the prophecy spoke about, The Messiah?
I could feel in Jesus his response was to laugh out loud at such thought, and he is searching for the words to convey his reaction!
Jesus: Now, within my whole essence, that if I was permitted, how can I answer such a grand question! How can I answer you clearly, except to say if you were I would you feel this question to be answerable?

Questioners: No.
Jesus continues....

Jesus: When I had my life on this planet I was not without my demons. I was not the figure that has been portrayed, and so there was not as I could say one person who saw my essence as this prophecy (*A prophecy*) that was portrayed from the need to control the mass.

Even though there was such a following for Jesus, those who came to listen to him did not recognize him as "The Messiah". Perhaps this was because as Jesus says – " when I walked on this planet I walked as man, no greater, no lesser". So, void of grandeur, mental or physical, he could truly be part of his community. However, his death and its events led some to claim him as the prophesied Messiah.

Question: It has been written or said that you would spend time talking with religious leaders. What would you discuss with them?

Jesus: Many times I would ask for an audience with the leaders of the churches, because on my travels I met many peoples who understood many things, and they were without control or fear. They spoke from a timeless Spirit and wonderment.

But, the leaders who I spoke with were trying to dictate and control, this caused me confusion. Maybe blindly, I felt I could offer to them what I had learnt on my travels. I felt that to be a spiritual advisor *(with reference to the church leaders)* of many peoples, ones persona would be open to vast understandings within the world. But, I found this not to be, I became a thorn to these so called, "Spiritual Leaders".

Question: You have spoken before of healings and some of these were miraculous healings. When this began to happen did you understand what was happening?

Jesus: Now place yourself in a situation of fear allow yourself to be led by fear and not responding to your Spirit, you will become diseased, you will become alone!

But ,when your Spirit is lifted and you begin to feel the wonder of Creation that has made you, that fills you, you yourself are your greatest healer. And so people saw this as miraculous, but they were only awakening to their Spirit.

Question: Can you explain why there are stories of miracles, and can you explain why masses were touched by you?

Jesus: My joy was in having the freedom to talk to so many and to share with them what was in my heart.

Many people who were in disease whether the imbalance was mental or physical had given up on life. Many disliked and judged themselves too harshly. It is easier to judge oneself than to have others judge you.

So, for example, if a person had the disease of leprosy, they were banished from society- this was harsh- but the judgment they put on themselves was much harsher. They judged themselves to be unclean, unworthy and unwanted, and yet, all they had was a slight imbalance.

So when the words I spoke ignited a spark or the light within them, what occurred was their energy rose and became more balanced. The most wondrous results were because the person had fought so much against themselves they had nothing left. The wondrous results did not occur to those who hoped it may happen, but for the ones who were so broken *and* rose in their own power.

Question: It is said that you rose Lazarus from the dead. Is this true, and if so how was this possible?

Jesus: This man somehow had, for some reason or another known only to himself, created a situation where upon he could enter a type of disconnection from his body, you call this, I feel, a trance like state?

Questioners: Yes.

Jesus: This occurred to many, and many unfortunately were thought to be dead and would then be seen to be dead, their physical body would be treated as such *(They were buried alive).*
This man had created this state, for what reason I am unaware of, but when I placed my hands upon him, I was simply feeling his body to see if it was warm. Maybe it was my timing to have been

69

there, as my hands touched him, his persona simply awakened!

My feelings were that this man was somewhat overly impressed and his excitement created a confused excitement with those around him and so my being was hailed in glory, but this was no miracle.

Question: It has been written that you challenged all people to be righteous, was this true what you asked of people, and what did you mean by this?

Jesus: My words were spoken to all who would listen, and when I spoke to those who listened their hearts spoke back to me. And so the light and freedom that would be produced and expand from all these people opened their hearts to hear that fear did not have a place in the house of God.

Question: There was a story that you came across a person that was to be stoned for adultery, and that you stopped this happening. Could you explain how you did this?

Jesus: The story you talk of was a story that occurred many times, many occasions people would chose to slight others that they felt had performed unrighteous acts of existence. But the people who chose to pick up the stones with ALL their hearts threw their pain and distaste of their own life towards the sufferer!

And so I would say to take that stone, hold that stone and CRUSH the stone with your own fear, for not believing in the light that emanates from your Soul. Only a person in immense darkness could do such an act (*to slight others*).

And so, no one wanted to be in darkness, they wanted to believe their magnitude! So, quite simply they aimed their fear into the stone and their hearts crumbled (*and their hearts became open once more to Creation*), and they became free!

Question: And what did you say to the person?

Jesus: But there were many, the one who was the target I would honor them and show all these people that this person *(the slighted)* has not judged, so who is free? He who judges, or he who is without judgment?

Question: Can you tell us if you had previously incarnated on this planet before, some believe you had?
Jesus: Your question comes from words that do not have any power.

Jesus' words indicated that untruths surrounded the presumption that he had incarnated before. Dismissing as always the false words and concepts of his life and of his Spirit without giving them power.

Question: Could I ask about the last supper, it is said that you withdrew from talking to the crowds and you would spend time with your friends *(disciples)* teaching them for when you leave. Could you explain what happened and if you left them any instructions?
Jesus: My words at our last gathering were of reassurance, and most importantly of simplicity. To remind them that they must always live their lives to the wonderment of their own life. They had many gifts between them all, but they were shrouded in fear. Fear to be free thinkers, fear that they must not question everything. I shared with them, feelings of great love for my fellow men. But, they wanted more they could not see that everything is so simple. One cannot be taught, one can only expand as one lets go of all their restricting thought forms. Each individual is their greatest teacher.

And yet we look to others to guide us. We can share similarities, and we can be comfortable with each other. But for all of us as individuals, we must learn from within. For when you have fully understood from within you find the peace and wonderment that is waiting for you.

Question: If you saw their fear did you know there would be a lot of confusion after you left?

Jesus: When I walked this planet there was much confusion, as I sit here tonight the confusion is calm. But beyond this space *(the room we were all gathered in)* the confusion still exists. Confusion is not negative because if one is not confused, then one will not know what peace is.

Question: Did you instruct those present at the Last Supper to "go and share your words"?

Jesus: I honor the individual integrity of every single person throughout time, then and now. And I honor that integrity and so it is not for me to control anyone's way of living.

Question: Did you, during that evening, predict that you would arise, after your death, and show yourself to them?

From the very core of his being, Jesus answers this question with unbridled passion. His Spirit growing in strength and spark as he recalls his deepest and firmly spoken words of assurance which he gave to his friends (who have become known as disciples) at the last supper.......

Jesus: Always I knew my Spirit was endless....... Always! And so the answer to this question is correct. I shared with my friends the understanding that the Spirit is endless;

"I WILL SHOW YOU MY WHOLE ESSENCE, AND I WILL SHOW YOU MY WOUNDS, AND I WILL SHOW YOU THAT MY HEART REMAINS AS ONE WITH GOD, AND THIS IS MY LEGACY."

This was to show them that there was nothing that could ever harm or destroy my essence.

Silence ensued for a short while as the group digested this powerful answer.

The session continues.......

Question: Can you explain what happened at your trial with Pontius Pilate?

Jesus calmly recalls the events of his trial.......

Jesus: There was much anger but the anger was from the leaders of the churches, because many were choosing not to be controlled by the false words and fears. Many people were beginning to become free in Spirit. This produced an uncomfortable effect for the churches. So, it was deemed that I as a speaker should be therefore cast away. This was more as an example.

Question: It is depicted that Pontius Pilate was almost trying to save you?

As Jesus' memory becomes clearer I could see a Roman Official sat casually in a rather elaborate chair flanked by around six or seven Roman soldiers. Directly facing this official was Jesus, and to Jesus' left, three or four irate men sporting long beards and head garments, appropriate to their profession as leaders of the churches. The official, (who I surmised was Pilate) appeared rather bored at the ranting of these leaders, as they presented their argument.

The Roman official seemed to be more concerned with keeping the church leaders; dare I say calm, as the leaders demanded judgment on Jesus. There appeared to be a form of pacification from the Roman quarters. Agreeing to cooperate with the church leaders suited the Romans as this would keep the churches reasonably satisfied. Such pacification made it easier for Roman rule to be maintained in a foreign country.

Jesus: There was a slight request that I should be spared, this is so. But, had I been saved then great disharmony would have occurred on both sides. And it was needed that the churches were portrayed as still being in control of the lands.

Question: I wanted to ask please, there is some confusion surrounding the crucifixion. Some people believe you did not die, that you survived and actually left Israel and went to possibly

India, is this true?

Jesus: I cannot defend what is not so. I walked this planet as you walk now. I often walked without clarity. I was a man, a friend, a son. I had no mystical powers. My essence departed from this earthly existence as my body weakened. With all the force left in my weakened body, I called to my Father;

"WITH ALL YOUR LOVE AND GLORY SEE IT UPON THE TRUTH OF MANKIND AND RELEASE THEM FROM THE PAIN AND SUFFERING THAT IS DROWNING THEIR SPIRIT."

My life ended, and yet my freedom began.[8]

Jesus' Unconditional Love For Mankind

Is was through the crucifixion that Jesus, despite the crippling agony of physical and emotional pain, became whole. That is to say Jesus experienced the nucleus of wholeness where no man, woman or child, no creature, no plant, no sea, no mountain; nothing is separated from God/Divine Will/Universal Flow or whatever title is given to the great energy that embodies EVERYTHING.

In this explosion of understanding Jesus' entire senses became saturated with the mass Soul filled pain and suffering that tormented mankind. A pain so deep, that erupted with the killing of another.

Mankind was lost, wild, scared and desperate. Tears poured from my eyes as Jesus spoke of this intense suffering of man that was racking his body and Soul. With Jesus' last breath's he held mankind's suffering deep in his heart. As he did so, Jesus' Spirit emanated an incredible comfort, love and understanding for all mankind, a feeling beyond description. He saw their glory through all his pain. Silence fell over him, as he was consumed by this love, freeing his Spirit from his now lifeless body.

Question: And it is said that you died with two others, I believe one was a murderer and one was a robber.

---

8. With this statement Jesus confirmed that his physical life ended upon the cross.

Jesus: Are you asking my essence this question?

Questioner: This is what the story says, that you died with two others on the cross?

Jesus: My death was an event that was solitary.

It was made clear to the people that the killing of Jesus should be as an example, and so his death was solitary to give warning to anyone else who dared publicly contest the ways of the churches.

Question: There is much spoken at present for your love for Mary Magdalene. This must have caused a lot of confusion when people saw you both together because of the judgments placed upon her. What happened, how did you meet each other?

Puzzled, Jesus replies …

Jesus: So you say many were confused by the relationship we began as one, but why would you ask such a question?

Question: Because in the writings it explains that the people were confused because you asked Mary Magdalene to wash your feet, and this shocked people because of her life.

Jesus: When my essence and the essence of my very dear, dear, dearest Mary became as one there was no confusion at all. Here was a lady who had suffered at the hands of many men. And yet she still found it within her heart to trust, so how can one be confused when such beauty from the heart is experienced.

From this heartfelt response to the memory of "Mary of Magdalene", I could feel Jesus marvel at her untarnished innocence to freely give her heart - considering the mental and physical abuse she had endured in the hands of others. It was through Mary's' love that Jesus could not only feel, but see the hope for all mankind. It was his encompassing respect for her stoical Spirit that fuelled his love for her.

Mary loved Jesus deeply, her love for him has never faltered. This was what I sensed, and what she projected from her Spirit, when she

75

communicated and shared her most intimate feelings during this channeled session.

Question: It is written that when you were talking to Nicodemus, you were said to say; "if one is not born of water and Spirit one cannot enter the Kingdom of God?" Some say, in this you were referring to Baptism. What did you actually mean, if you did say it?

Jesus: I choose not to acknowledge your statement.

Again, Jesus' lack of acknowledgement deems this to be false.

Question: Having been born as the Son of God, why did you have to be baptized, was this symbolic or was there another reason for this?

Jesus: My life up to the point of my baptism was somewhat wild! I sowed my seeds, I drank, I was outspoken. I would not bow down and conform to the false words that were being spoken. My Spirit was strong. I was a man in all senses. I lived my life to the full with great pleasure up to the time of my "baptism". So many knew my past and it was from my past that I could draw many strengths from. If I had not lived as a man, and fulfilled my role as a man, then how could I understand man!

So I lived and I lived well, my cousin *(John)* was also *(in youth)* quite wild! We knew others were seeing us as "now untarnished" because we had both stepped forward to do my Fathers work and so "baptism" was the only way for us to reach the people. They held within them chains of their past ways that they could not release and so to baptize, to clean with water, to wash away was the task I showed them all.

It was for my essence to remind those of my wild ways of living and to declare that from this day forward my heart and Soul would walk with my Father.

They *(the people)* had been ingrained with dark and false words. They were told they had "sinned," they were in "dirt," they were "unclean," they will never have continued life because they were "Soul-less", they were told they are lesser than the creatures that walk in the Earth. And these people believed the words of these false priests. [9]

So, the only way was to show a simplicity, and that simplicity was to be baptized. They were convinced they were to be consumed in darkness. Many knew I also had been wild, this knowing enabled me to "lead" the way *(to wash away the wildness of my youth).* As water washes outwardly they could see how, by full immersion of the body and honoring God, their Spirit would rise renewed by the ever cleansing and life affirming waters.

Question: There was also a suggestion that you spoke of Hell and Heaven and of the Soul and the body being destroyed in Hell, what did you mean?

Jesus: Now one statement that I would make and make constantly would be to share with many that; "if you place your Soul within fear and you choose fear to rule your life then what place in God's Kingdom do you have? For God's Kingdom knows only joy and light."

Now I will answer one more question…..

Question: There was one other passage that says you speak of the importance to "love one another, love ones enemies and love God". What is the importance of these words, the importance of love?

Jesus: Quite simply, when you love you cannot be an aggressor, there is no room.

Balancing Self Doubt and Insecurities
Releasing and understanding replaced the confusion and fog that had previously been housed for many years in my mental,

---

9. Continued life: - Jesus meaning by this life after death, as the priest had told these people that their Spirit would not continue after their death.

emotional and spiritual levels. I had come to know and accept the Spirit of Jesus as a great friend. A friend who had stepped into my life, who truly understood the difficulties of physical life, whilst never losing sight of life's real meaning.

Life, that has been produced so magnificently within the mysterious workings of Creation, God and Universal Flow can at times seem so confusing. But, to see Jesus as the man he was, and not as history would dictate him to be, enriched my understanding of everyday living. Outwardly, my life appeared not to have changed at all. But, inwardly much clarity about my life had occurred. It was so refreshing to realize Jesus, during times in his life, also struggled to find clarity. Understanding Jesus' life helped me to be aware that we (often unknowingly) create our own obstacles and blocks in life. That we can make a conscious choice to step beyond our own self-limiting ways and try another route or direction in our journey through our life. How refreshing it was to learn that one does not need to follow the ways of another to be accepted by God, Creation, Universal Flow.

Of course, I was and still remain at times plagued by self-doubts and insecurities. But, now I feel a much greater inner strength and freedom to be myself and be true to my own path in life. I can now clearly recognize that these self-doubts are merely a mixture of the more negative aspect of my personality and pressures of social up bringing. When these "little monsters" pop up I know to take time to marvel at the syntheses of all things in creation. This helps to free me for a while from my personal struggles, expanding me mentally and spiritually into this newly vibrant colorful view of life. Holding such a view of Spring like freshness, infused with freedom and inner clarity, I am able to appreciate everyone I meet and understand their distinctive uniqueness respectfully.

The process of making the decision to consciously step away from my internal struggles, to slow down mentally and emotionally, sometimes takes a moment, sometimes a day, sometimes weeks or even months. With perseverance, these times of struggle do pass. As each struggle passes, it is replaced with a greater sense of clarity and appreciation for life and creation, and for a time a feeling of being empowered.

9

Final Meeting

"You Will Live Always"

Word had spread in my local community of my meetings with the spirit of Jesus, and of the questions put to his essence. The answers given in these sessions brought about an interest from a number of people who were practicing Christians. People who, though very respected in the Christian community, had quietly questioned the accuracies of the Bibles' New Testament. These people were hoping for an opportunity to ask Jesus of these inaccuracies.

The synchronicities of our lives coming together made this meeting possible. Jesus' Spirit was impressing on my psyche that this would be the final meeting for now, and that once this meeting was over Jesus would have shared the truth of his life and his Spirit would be freed. (As I wrote these words a butterfly flew into my home!)

This was to be the most powerful of all the meetings, powerful in the content of questions and powerful in Jesus' responses'. In fact, when this meeting ended all the lights in my house short-circuited, so intense was Jesus' presence.

Peter: I am the one who all you know, and I am now much freer in my existence. For so, so, so, *(long)* I have walked with great burdens and great darkness. But, my Spirit and my essence begins now to shine in freedom and glory and for this I give many, many, many, many, many, many joys to mankind.

I am known as the friend who walked so long ago with the one whom many praise. My name is of Peter. I come because I feel there are some confusions as to certain written events of sometimes of great power. I come in freedom and joy.

Questioners: Welcome Peter.

Question: Peter, there was an occasion which we call the Transfiguration, it is said Jesus had taken you, James and John up to a high place where Jesus transformed into a shiny white figure; Moses and Elijah appeared and a voice was heard saying;

"This is my beloved son in whom I am well pleased". You wrote about this in one of your letters to the early Christians and it also appears in three of the Gospels in the New Testament?

Peter: Now I can bring forth this event of which you speak. It is so my friend...... and always I *(emphasizing I)* would address my friend as my Master. I now know this form of inner worship became a burden for my friend. So, through my understanding I have chosen to refer to my friend simply as Jesus.

We all went one sun-filled vibrant day in our lives to this place of which you speak. We were all light in Spirit sharing stories of our childhood, my Spirit would raise in light the essence of my friend Jesus, I would say "but you know all, you know everything, why do we have these times to share -you know everything." This was an element from my essence of, many may say, trying to place down my friend's Spirit.

Peter feels heavily burdened as he recalls his mocking type banter towards his friend. He seemed to have had some type of resentment of Jesus' clarity, along with his undoubtedly magnetic and passionate personality. Peter feeling uncomfortable with himself lowers his head in humbleness as he is himself confronted with his imbalanced feelings towards his friend at times.

Peter continues...................

Peter: My Spirit must now undo the great wrong that my imbalanced nature caused *(This was said with extreme firmness as Peter called on his inner strength and truth to speak bravely and clearly.)*

And so with much strength I now declare this statement that so many have founded so many beliefs upon *(Talking softly, his Spirit calming to surrender of the truth within him).*

81

was not so.

Peter explains further detailing his part in the story, he becomes strong and clear in his words, as his dormant bravery surfaces ....

Peter: I knew that by reporting such an image my essence would become great, so burdened was I that I walked in my mind in the shadow of my friend, for so long I could not choose to see the greatness that was his Spirit.

Peter was full of great remorse at his sometimes rather brash behavior towards his friend. Knowing he did not intentionally mean to have such a loose tongue, but nevertheless he allowed his small irritations to surface, as he witnessed the love and support that Jesus received from many people.

Having delivered his statement his courage lessened as he is filled with deep regret. He judges his exaggerated accounts harshly resulting with heaviness now in his Spirit. Feeling unworthy to continue, Peter becomes silent and embarrassed at his past.

The group do not pick up the intensity of Peter's feelings and gently asked the following question which, after a few minutes, finally brought Peter out of his self inflicted apathetic condition.

Question: May I ask you another question?

There was a lack of response from Peter. Undeterred the group member gently continues to ask.........

Question: On one occasion you and another of Jesus' friends had been talking about what people had been saying about Jesus and you said to him; "Many of them think you might be one of the prophets who have come back again." and Jesus is said to have said to you;

"But who do YOU think I am?"

It is then written that you Peter immediately said;

"You are the Messiah the son of the living God."

With which Jesus replied;

"Because this truth has been revealed to you, you will be the rock on which my church is founded."

Do you recognize this occasion?

Peters Spirit continues to be greatly traumatized. He drops his head further as he recalls this occasion, feeling unworthy somehow to speak from his heart. Yet to access his heart and acknowledge all his weaknesses he knows is the only way he can right these miswritten events that have steered many away from the truth of his friend. He answers now with shaken strength and responsibility, as if his previously felt courage and bravery had become diluted.

Peter: My answer was so. *(Recognizing the occasion).* But my answer was to mock my friend *(sighs deeply)*. My whole essence was imbalanced by my great ego! But you ask for the response of my friend; *(ensuing love now flows through Peter's Spirit as he remembers the heartfelt response from Jesus to him)* my friend simply placed his hand on my heart and said;

"You Peter hold so much within your Spirit, and yet your Spirit will one day set many free."

Peter's ego internally exaggerated this response, which in turn inflated his ego further and so his inner truth could not feel what Jesus actually meant by this.

As a group we all could feel Peter's traumatized Spirit, taking responsibility for the truth whilst facing his previous exaggerations. We could sense from Peter the lasting spiritual heaviness connected with reporting something or someone inaccurately to make ourselves look good. Peter's earthly actions gave us all an insight to the negative power of false words!

Peter courageously steps beyond his self-imposed judgment to speak once more, feeling stronger and lighter in his Spirit as he does so.....

Peter: And now through my pain and my imbalances, I know the way to freedom is to find your truth within. Your truth that your ego cannot deny.

AND I PETER VOW FOR ALL OF CREATION THAT I, FROM THIS TIME

FORWARD WILL ONLY WALK TO THAT TRUTH.

Questioners: Thank you Peter.

Peter bows low to the group before he departs. With ease Peters' Spirit leaves my body, whilst my head is maneuvered backwards to "open" to the next Spirit. Immediately, I recognized the familiarity of the entering Spirit........

Questioners: Welcome.

Jesus: I am the one you know as the Master Jesus. I am Yeshua. I come to answer many of your somewhat probing questions and concerns. I come forth within this moment to embrace you all within my heart. I ask that within your hearts also you embrace my essence as you would the most innocent of babes.

Now we can share.

Questioners: Thank you.

Question: You tell us Jesus that you came into the world as a man like any of us -"no greater no lesser". But, at what stage in your life did you became aware that it was your mission to disseminate the Christ Spirit in the world?

Jesus: My *(true)* task was never revealed whilst I walked on this planet. So to know my Soul task was to ground within the structure of the blessed Earth and so into all mankind the Christ Light, The Christ Energy as you call this, I was unaware. It was only on my passing, as I transcended from my pained body *(Jesus' breath began to still as his memory recalled the sense of wonder that he experienced as his Spirit left his physical body, this sense once again filling his entire essence)* that I could see this immense glow occurring on the planet and within the hearts of all. It was a moment where I truly transcended into my Fathers house and eternal life.

Question: Can you explain how you came to believe it was an important part of your mission that you should be put to death?
Jesus: Not once did I believe, not once was I without fear, not once was my heart without pain, but throughout all of this my whole essence was filled with a conviction, a knowing that this is so. Not once did I know why, not once did I feel judged, but not once did I deny my Fathers Spirit and love. And so, through my pain I knew that all was as it should be.

Question: Did you have any expectations that your followers the Apostles, or whatever you would like to call them were going to carry on your work after your death?
Jesus: My work as you so ask, was not to continue. My life had been spent sharing great wisdoms and understandings with many. But, these were not only my understandings, but these were the ways that my Father worked. My Father is not only within my essence, but within the essence of everyone and everything. And so not once did I even begin to understand my work would carry on; this was my Father's work, this was the work of ALL of Creation.

My Father resides in everyone and everything.

Question: Did you truly deliver the basic teaching of the Sermon on the Mount, which comes to us through the gospel of St. Matthew, which includes the Lords Prayer? Though you have indicated that you did not come to found a church, most of us in the west have been nurtured within what we call the Christian tradition. Our great difficulty is to know what to believe?
Jesus: When I walked the planet there were many times that I would talk, and many sermons I would give. There were times

when events had caused much distress within the people and it would be at these times I would offer words of calmness, the words I would speak on many occasions would be……..

"OUR GREAT FATHER WHO RESIDES IN ALL THAT IS SEEN AND THAT CANNOT BE SEEN.

OUR GREAT FATHER WHO HEARS THE UNSPOKEN WORDS AND THE WORDS THAT ARE SPOKEN, HEAR OUR HEARTS, HEAR OUR SOULS CALL OUT TO YOU.

BRING US LIGHT BRING US PEACE.

WITH ALL YOUR GREAT LIGHT BESTOW UPON US ALL THE GIFT OF REST AND CALM.

TAKE US ALL INTO YOUR HOUSE, RESIDE OUR SPIRITS WITHIN YOU AND GRANT US ALL GREAT WISDOM TO SEE BEYOND THE PAIN AND SUFFERINGS THAT OCCUR WITHIN ALL PEOPLES.

HEAR US AND HEAR OUR CALL."

Question: May I ask one question about our beliefs. You have told us about your concern over the inaccuracies in the writings about you in the New Testament and elsewhere. Many Christians have doubts about the truth and even some of the most fundamental beliefs like the claim that you were conceived by the Holy Spirit and born of the Virgin Mary.

But, they can still go on believing in you and your mission here, so in the end do these inaccuracies really matter?
Jesus: Now we have two questions one we have the question upon churches is that not your question?
Questioners: Yes.

Jesus: So my answer is this; many churches and man's beliefs have been based upon my life, but not my life as I lived it. Many have been based upon the words of others and many peoples have been understanding that to become free to live in the Kingdom of my Father they must adhere to some religions is that not so?

Questioners: Yes.

Jesus: But, when I passed *(Jesus' life ended)* there became a great sense of freedom in the hearts of many and the freedom simply was the Christ Energy or the Christ Light, the Great Spirit igniting in power within those who would listen.

Within your question you asked of the Spirits of many who adhere to a so-called conformed structure of Christianity. Will my words create waves, will my words bring down those foundations, will Christianity suffer because my presence is here sharing with you the truth of my life, is that not your question?

Question: Yes, could there be great harm in people understanding that their cherished beliefs are not so, is it better to leave them with their cherished beliefs?

Jesus: For many they will repulse the words that I speak now, *(voice softens)* but for many their hearts and Spirits have longed for this freedom and it is those who are ready to step forward in light that my Father cannot deny any more. And so it is those great Spirits who still conform to Christianity and yet in their hearts and Souls they know Christianity is just a "house," it has limitations. They know this is just a small aspect of belief, for those people, their Spirits will be set free.

And so we then look at the ones who will repulse my words. They will shudder and renounce what is being said in this moment. Many renounced my words when I walked the planet, and so by my essence coming forward in these times to share with you, then there is great freedom that is occurring. Does this answer your question?

Universal Flow/ Creation/ God could not flow freely through set beliefs. Once the individual became free of dogma, Universal Flow/ God and All of Creation could expand with the light of those returning home. This is what Jesus meant by…. "My Father cannot deny anymore".

Questioner: Yes.

Question: When you walked on the planet did you ever have psychic or paranormal experiences, such as seeing Angels, visions, people who had died, awareness of other dimensions, Spirit Guides or visions of the future?

Jesus: My life when I walked as man contained many images of which you speak. I was blessed with what many would see as further understanding. To say could I foretell the future was not so, but I would see the great lights and great energies coming forth towards my Spirit and often this would enhance the words I spoke when I walked the planet. I feel at many times during the great sermons my whole essence would be taken over by a great power, this was always how I would see my Father.

Question: We all talk about "Our Father in Heaven," should we be thinking more of an unimaginable power who cannot be referred to just in terms as a personal figure like a father?

Jesus sighs deeply.......

Jesus: Your essence holds much wisdom. Indeed, we are so small on this planet and our Father so great. But, even within our whole essence we cannot possibly understand the greatness "Our Father" is. And so it is a fine way to understand the Spirit of ALL as Our Father.

Question: Many religious teachings at the time you walked the Earth recommended fasting, meditation, circumcisions and celibacy as a means to cleanse the body. Did you ever recommended such practices?

Jesus: I warm at your question and I warm because this is a way to cleanse ones self, not so much as the meditation of which you speak. Stillness is far greater and the stillness I speak about is the life you are given. To become still within, to appreciate your life without all your struggles and your turmoil's, without all your wants and needs and desires. Appreciate the air as a breath upon your skin, as the light within. To feel the smallest leaf as a great consciousness, to feel how blessed you are to be given life and Soul.

This you can achieve through stillness and remembering you are a small, small heart within the Greatness.

Now you talk of fasting, this was indeed a great way to achieve rebalance. Often, for my essence to regain the experience of re-centering, I would choose to fast. But, fasting did not necessarily mean all foods and liquids, only retraction of the foods and liquids that I constantly over took. Does that make an understanding for you?

Questioner: Thank you.

Question: Can you tell us if you had a special relationship with God that perhaps we ordinary mortals don't have?
Jesus: My answer is the relationship I have with my Father YOU have also. But, within your Spirit is the need to grow and understand more of this dimension, and so your access to the relationship with your Father, with my Father, is perhaps somewhat lessened. But, your relationship is ultimately as powerful as mine.

Question: Can God be found in the other great religions such as Islam and Buddhism?
Jesus: All teach the same, but under a different structure. The blocks that occur are because the minds of man take teachings with far too much rigidity. They hear only words and do not allow their Spirit to move beyond those words. One must remember organized religions contain "must do's and must be's." My Father only knows ONENESS FOR ALL. My Father contains no "must do's or must be's," my Father simply **IS**.

Question: Is there any truth in some of the ancient religions, say, the Greeks with all their Gods, Zeus and Mars and these beings which seem to have been invented?

Jesus: All these as you call them "Gods" are aspects of my great Father. They are ALL powerful and they ALL have their rightful place within my Fathers energy. Not one is separate, but due to the cultural understanding that different peoples have, (this) has therefore created limitation in the flow of these energies.

Question: What is meant by what we call Heaven?

This answer was given with hypnotic softness......

Jesus: Heaven as man sees it is a grand time for the Spirit to rest and feel nurtured.

Heaven truly exists. Heaven is real, Heaven is a place within my Father where one is nurtured like the tiniest, softest feather that has fallen from the Soul of the greatest light, and so requires peace and nurturance. Heaven is a place of great comfort, where Spirits will find the strength that is needed once more to walk their path into light and freedom.

Question: Some who have lived lives of great wickedness would not be admitted to Heaven?

Jesus: You make such great judgment. My Father holds no separation, but there is an area beyond the Heavens where burdened and pained spirits will need to enter to cast aside their great imbalances and chains.

Question: When we die do we continue to live in a spiritual state?

Jesus: Your question is rather small, to answer your question in fullness would only be possible when you do not need physical life anymore (*indicating our limited comprehension of the workings of the Universal Flow and God, whilst in the physical body*).

But, a small answer I shall give........

Many will enter the Heavens, but there are a few who will go beyond the Heavens, for already they walk this planet in absolute light, therefore their essences will move to where they are, symbolically speaking, required next.

Question: Have you had any communication with the founders of other religions like Mohammed (peace be upon him), or Gautama Buddha?

Jesus: Many structures or religions are based on one thing, one belief and that is eternal life. Eternal life **IS** my Father. And so to answer your question would only have my Spirit coming from the mind's of man.

Question: Can you tell us something about your resurrection? We are told that three days after your death you are said to have left the tomb in which your body was lain and appeared in bodily form to your followers. You showed them the marks of the nails in your hands and feet, you even took meals with them, but then you would disappear as suddenly as you had appeared?

Jesus: My passing caused great trauma to many. Many became fearful and many became lost. Many saw me as a leader and on my passing to see their leadership slaughtered in such a way left many without hope. There became much confusion and anguish many began to renounce the words I shared.

I could feel waves of storm like emotional and mental thunder, pain, loss and confusion sweep over the land shortly after Jesus' death.

Jesus: Many became lost in such darkness, and so my essence came forward with much strength (*speaking with firm projection and direction*) to present my body to these tormented people, but not in such physical bones and blood but through their pain and fear and renouncement of all, to show them that I am still here. And so, many wrote that I returned and quite simply this is because I HAD NEVER GONE, MY BODY WAS EMPTY BUT MY SPIRIT IS FULL.

And so their reports, slightly unbalanced, were true because this is how they saw me.

I could sense from Jesus' memory the enormous effort it took for his Spirit to be shown to these people. He could see them becoming almost permanently lost in their darkness, not understanding the concept of eternal life.

Even in death Jesus would not leave them pained and tormented. The projection of his Spirit to them lifted any doubts of his words and eternal life. This vision empowered all those who saw him.

For witnessing a paranormal event does appear at the time to be more "real" than physical life experiences. One's intellect automatically becomes quiet, as the undeniable paranormal experience envelopes the individual and time seems to stand still.

Question: At the feast of Pentecost Luke tells us of the coming of the Holy Spirit to your followers. In his account all the believers were gathered together when suddenly there was a noise and a strong wind and the sky was filled with what looked like tons of fire which touched them all and filled them with the Holy Spirit and it began to speak in the many languages of the people who were there for the feast of Pentecost. Is this an event which you recognize?

Jesus: You ask of the Holy Spirit which is the only part of your question I shall acknowledge. (*Not acknowledging the incident suggests that this was not an occasion in which Jesus was part of*).

Divine wonder begins to fill Jesus' Spirit as he describes to us the Holy Spirit....

Jesus: The Holy Spirit is the great essence that resounds through my Father. The great heartbeat that is my Father. My Father is the Power of Creation, but my Father in his power is filled with the Holy Spirit, just as you now are filled with your Spirit.

The Holy Spirit is the Great Consciousness that is my Father.

Question: May I ask you a question about the Saul of Tarsis known later as Paul. He is supposed to have been miraculously converted from being a persecutor of your followers into a believer of you one day on his way to Damascus. Was this an event which took place?

Jesus: I cannot answer this. But I can say that the being you know as Paul became somewhat imbalanced. His life before was quite "heavy", but seemingly he began to see the lights shining in the eyes of many he met. The lights that shone through the eyes of these strangers began to diffuse his heavy path but, as with many, there were many things he misread. And so that is all I shall make comment on.

Question: Just one more thing about Paul that has been said, that he was the greatest influence of spreading Christianity to the wider world, but that he was very judgmental in his opinions?

Jesus: Christianity as a religion is not something in my essence that I feel I would like to acknowledge too much. Because it does not speak truly of my life.

My life was with many people great wonder, but my life was not separate from Creation, and Christianity creates great separation. My Father holds no judgment.

Question: We've been asking you very deep matters, may I now ask you something of a slightly lighter nature. You told us you were somewhat unruly as a child so we know you had a sense of fun. Did you retain your sense of humor when you reached the serious time of your life? Were there times when you could laugh and be merry with your disciples / friends?

Jesus: My life within all its time held many occasions of wonder, so yes I was as a child and in my youthful times rather unruly, my Spirit was strong and my spirit was full of renouncing of all judgmental deeds. After I had studied *(from Jesus' memory, the study period of his life was when he spent time with the Essene broth-*

erhood) my life and all that I could see became immersed in wonder. And so with my friends, my closest, it is so that I spent many empowering times of great joy. Times that were filled not just with mere laughter but with great wonder at all around me, and this became my passion and so the art of being serious was not so, more passionate.

Question: They say that laughter is one of the greatest gifts that we've been given in this life and at times, even through sadness and trouble, it can be the greatest tonic for us?

Jesus: And so how many laugh? *(Feeling pain at the lack of laughter in mankind)*

How many......... but one must ask why has laughter become so silent? It has become silent because man has become so controlled by so many ways to think or do or be. This will begin to lift and once more laughter will be heard as the song that it was truly created in.

Now, I will answer a final question.

Question: If you had once again an opportunity to address mankind, what would You like to tell us all?

Jesus: I would simply say; remember all the wondrous things that you are individually capable of. The silent gifts that you do not speak of, the deep lovings that you feel for one another.

I would say; remember always you have life, each life supports your neighbor and your neighbor supports your life.

Do not empower yourself by casting aside your neighbor and your light, even when you doubt everything do not doubt your ability to.....breathe. For your breath contains your light and your right as part of Gods Kingdom.

And when your Spirit finally leaves your physical body know that you are merely beginning once more in greatness;

YOU WILL LIVE ALWAYS.

These words brought tears to my eyes as I transcribed Jesus' gentle and sincere words onto the computer. My heart was filled with a simplicity, a simplicity not forgotten but that had not been felt for a while. I looked out my window to my garden and felt an intensified wonder at the perfection that surrounds us all, as inside I became still.

Questioner: Thank you, can I ask how would you best like to be remembered?
Jesus responds with a deep outward breath, as if he was saying; "Do I need to be remembered by mankind, when we are ALL equal?" ......
Jesus: You ask how would my essence like to be remembered, but I say;

"How would you like to be remembered?"

Would you like to be remembered as one who suffered, or would you like to be remembered as the very source of light and hope, not only for yourself but for all mankind. If each one of you ALL remember in your Spirit YOU individually contain *(the very source of)* light and hope, for then you ARE set free.

Group members in turn thank Jesus.

Jesus takes a couple of minutes to honor Creation, Universal Flow, and God for enabling this session to take place. He bows low to the group before departing.

10

Karma and the Soul

"No energy upon this Earth,
no energy upon all Creation judges you except yourself"

Karma

During the years of channeling, before the Spirit of Jesus communicated, a number of people I met were questioning as to what karma was. The diversity in their understanding of the subject opened a dimensional doorway for a session to take place and give some answers to this vast law.

A being / energy enters and "he" introduces himself, I say "he" as the connection to this energy / Spirit felt considerably more masculine in nature.......

Questioners: Welcome.

Spirit: My task is to bring forth much knowledge of karma.
Questioners: Thank you.
Question: Could you explain and share what karma actually is?
Spirit: All who know on your planet of karma have begun to understand its very basic words. I, as one Lord of Karma come now to explain. Karma exists within this dimension and also within dimensions that are affected by your deeds here.

Many feel karma is based upon theory; what one does, so does it return. This is merely a form of justification. The physical form of karma which man often adheres to, is created solely for the ego; and the ego has control over many laws. But, all laws that exist within the physical karma have no place in the Universes.

Question: So, what actually is Karmic Law?

Karmic Lord: The Law of all Karma is growth of man's Soul. Some are aware and some are yet to become aware. The Soul of man does not exist within this planet the Soul has been created by ....All

Whenever a being / energy refers to "All", unconditional love, an honoring, a feeling that cannot be verbally expressed is contained in a moment of silence. As the being / energy acknowledges the magnitude and intelligence that is the limitless power of the Ultimate Force. Many beliefs refer to this Force as God, Great Spirit, the Source, or a similar relevant title native to ones mass cultural or personal belief.

As the silence lifts the Karmic Lord continues ....

And all experiences that man shares and learns by upon this planet, assist to help the Soul grow, and so this is given the word karma; and this is what in my being and many other Lords of Karma, we refer to as karma.

As the Karmic Lord shared this information, I could experience the meaning of karma and the effect karma has on the physical. This type of karma is not acknowledged by the Karmic Lords, since physical karma is born out of ego and therefore holds no spiritual growth. The Karmic Lords acknowledge "true karma", which is when we ourselves under-stand our creation of an unjustified deed. We begin to feel burdened by the imbalance of these actions, our Soul does not feel free and our Spirit cries out for help.

This tormented realization of our individual past ego-fuelled imbal-ances, opens gateways within the individual psyche enabling the Lords of Karma to step in. A situation is then created in life for us to under-stand and learn the origins of the motives that led us to perform such unhealthy deeds.

These learning times do not necessarily mean for example; if you were to shoot someone, you will have to get shot in return, for your previous negative action to be free of that particular karma. Indeed, for

many the sheer remorse of one's actions is enough to set them free. Although they will not perhaps feel this freedom, until they find themselves a way to give back to society and the world what they "took out". This it seems is a personal quest that the individual would have taken on to not only (symbolically speaking) rebalance the scales, but often becomes an event where they end up giving far more than was Universally required.

The session continues....

Question: Bearing in mind that every action has a reaction, what are the criteria you use to ascertain whether an individual karma is a 'credit' or 'debit' karma?

Karmic Lord: Now I ask, within your question is there a request for the person to be judged?

Question: Yes, a means of judging?

Karmic Lord: As a Karmic Lord I can now share with you..... (*The following said with strength and clarity*) No energy upon this Earth, no energy upon all Creation judges you except yourself. And so your karma, of which you all speak, that seemingly governs mankind, is brought forth from a judgment from mankind.

And so if, shall we say, you felt you caused pain to your neighbor and this burden was carried deep within your heart, the only way for your Soul to grow would be to release this burden. You yourself chooses to release such a burden. Often you may choose to experience an act of great harm to yourself. In many ways, it would be wiser to offer light and acknowledgement to the person acting as a catalyst (the person or situation that has released you from your burden) and in doing so freeing your heart and allowing your Spirit to grow, and so your Soul becomes more and more.

I shall explain........many deeds upon this planet are performed; and often they are performed in an un-light manner. Many people begin to judge "this is karma and so it will come back"; and yet if, within the being or within the being's Soul they felt they truly performed no wrong then no karma has been created. And this is because the being has not judged himself. But, it is the task of all Lords of Karma to place such a being within a situation similar, but not so drastic, so they may understand their deed.[10]

Question: But would you say the motive is more important than the deed?

Karmic Lord: My task is to assist all children who are led to such ways by thoughts of negativity and power, and also by entities that choose to enter onto your planet through a weakness of the child or children. My task, and of many others, is to assist in releasing those children of those burdens. And so "motive" is often caused by influence of energies of an un-light nature. For when the Spirit truly sings there are always no motives, only peace, no sense of achievement, only peace. Throughout all your daily lives, when one strives to achieve more, one forgets they have the most potent gift our Father can give, and that is LIFE, and yet, how many people ....LIVE?

Question: Can I ask about attitudes in relation to karma?

Karmic Lord: All of you are as worthy as the most profound person you may choose to see on your planet. But, in your minds eye, if you choose you have greater knowledge or greater wisdom than your neighbor, then this is attitude; and so when you experience your own attitudes (for those who do not have conscious access to these Boards) you can ask, before you enter

---

10. Some people may feel somewhat deflated and sad to think that there is no judgment from Creation placed on those who have done "bad" things during their life. That they are not made to pay a big debt to those they have pained and hurt. There is no value to be gained in Judgment, but much to be gained by all for an individual to truly learn. And so Creation will help to place each person in the most appropriate conditions for them to learn.

your sleep state, that you may go to the Boards of Karma and face these entities. Much then will be learnt by you. Always we are willing to help, but the greatest obstacle you have now on your planet is of your immense attitudes.

Question: Where do these attitudes stem from?
Karmic Lord: These attitudes will always stem from present life and from past lives. It is a most powerful process for each person to perform when they depart from this planet, to feel that they are Spirit and not look back at what they have achieved, but to remember the true joys that living brought them. This very simple process will allow the Spirit to become free of burden.

If when you die your last thoughts are, as one example; "I could have done more," then you carry much heaviness with you to the world beyond. But one memory of light is enough to free the Soul.

Question: Speaking of life, what are the karmic connotations for England and the English people when we have accepted legalized abortion, which I feel is a contradiction of natural selection?
Karmic Lord: Now you ask of the laws that many peoples in many countries are creating, which are turning its backs on nature.

The Karmic Lord becomes quiet as a great sadness floods his energy, his voice becomes softer as he speaks very gently......

If man loses his Spirit to all controlling ways, then man will be no more. But, every child on this planet knows consciously the answer to your question, and yet all excuses to rise above nature and becoming all-controlling silences mans' intuition. But, also man needs to see how far he can go? But, I can tell you Divine Plan changes, and as Divine Plan changes, if beings do not follow such changes, once more man shall not be.

Many peoples upon your planet have begun to work logically and logic is a tool for the ego. The ego is fine when in balance, but right now upon your planet many are always wanting to "prove".

Very, very rarely do they follow inside. *(Touches heart)*. There is a need, a false need, to be highly successful, materially motivated, and so you push your children and you push yourselves. And yet, in nature what grows naturally lasts.

Questioners: Thank you.
Karmic Lord: Now I shall depart.

The Difference Between the Soul & the Spirit

The Soul is the source of an individual's spiritual energy. It is a source (along with Creation and Universal Flow) that is continually expanding in strength and power. As the Spirit incarnates into new life, many challenging situations in life and within the self are faced. These are aspects within our physical, mental, emotional and spiritual selves.

It is our individual struggles and triumphs that enable our Soul to grow in strength and power. The Soul is literally our "powerhouse". The Earth is at present a great school for learning and acceptance of the human Spirit and Soul. The Spirit is an aspect of the individual's higher self (also known as our Angelic Self). We are a fraction of our individual Spark in which we were created.

Our Angelic Self, our spark, is far too intense a vibration to exist as a whole on this planet. So, quite simply, a fragment is released from our "whole self" into the newly created physical form. As we enter new life on Earth, we are surrounded by a protective energy that we call an Aura. The Aura becomes, symbolically speaking, a photo album. As we move through life, images (mental and emotional memories) begin to fill this album. When death arrives at our door, our Aura, along with the tiny fragment of our whole Angelic Self, unite to enter the "Heavens," also known as the Astral Realms, to reflect upon the life that has been lived. The uniting of the two becomes recognizable as the Spirit. Therefore, the Spirit is a combination of the Aura, along with the projected fragment of the individual's whole Angelic Self or spark.

Since the Aura is our mental and emotional "photo album", it is possible to trace and retrieve certain experiences of our preceding life or lives held within our Aura. These are both experiences which helped to enhance our Soul growth; as well as certain mental, emotional and spiritual blocks that have been picked up and are preventing our Soul from expanding. Without the continued expansion of our Soul, our individual Self struggles to keep up with the ever expanding Universal Flow, Creation and God.

11

Conclusion

"I walked this planet as you walk now.
I often walked without clarity.
I was a man, a friend, a son.
I had no mystical powers"

There are those who either consciously or intuitively recognize that Jesus played a significant part in human evolution. Although many remain confused by historical and theological accounts of Jesus' existence and their explanation of the relevant importance of his life. For those people may not feel comfortable with such written explanations, yet deep within themselves they know his life was important, and so confusion occurs.

Jesus explained that; "For many they will repulse the words that I speak *(the words contained within this book)* but for many their hearts and Spirits have longed for this freedom and it is those who are ready to step forward in light that my Father cannot deny any more.... for those people, their Spirits will be set free."

Many will find answers to their confusions within these transcripts; those who prefer to live by the written word, rather than their own inner guidance, will have found the transcripts contents challenging. However, they may feel reassured that Jesus' life was indeed a very profound event in mankind's history. An event that surpasses all that has previously been written. For the culmination of Jesus' death upon the cross was indeed one of complete self sacrifice, one that allowed the grounding of the Christ Light and Energy on the Earth and into all life upon it. This was an event which truly saved mankind from self-destruction and remains as an unconscious memory within us all.

It seems many remain resistant to the perfection that they were created in and have a long way to go in acknowledging their "Spark", their Light and in that; their interconnection and interdependence with Creation and God.

The Christ Energy is a healing energy that exists within all peoples, cultures and denominations. It can be referred to as the "Light of the World" and is here to be ignited within all of us. One only has to ask for it to be ignited within them. It will assist our transformation. Our acknowledgement of this most pure energy within us is what Jesus referred to as the "second coming." He confirmed that he would not re-incarnate or have another physical life on Earth. "For man has long looked for another being to show him out of darkness, but the step must come from within."

Jesus explained that the "Kingdom of Heaven is the Soul of the Heart....For man to enter the Kingdom of Heaven... he must first find peace within and without; for when this has been achieved, he has found the Kingdom of Heaven." And so, the Christ Light and Energy is now grounded within us to light our way to the "Kingdom of Heaven", and assist in our enlightenment and reconnection to Creation / God and eternal life.

Jesus emphasized that he walked as a "brother" and not, as he is so often depicted, as a "Messiah" or "Chosen one". He confirmed that; "When I walked on the Earth Plane I walked with man and I walked as man – no greater, no lesser." He explained that he was "no magician" and that he came to show us we are all "true beings of light."

Yes, remarkable healings of mind and body did occur during Jesus' life. But, Jesus did not directly attribute these numerous mental and physical recoveries to himself. "Much of this did occur, but it was also the being who healed himself by acknowledging the Creator in his Soul. I merely could become a channel to open the heart of the child in question so they could also experience total oneness. Yes much occurred, but it came because the child was willing." It is understandable that many of those witnessing such cures (during a time in history where most had no formal education) – including his very closest of friends- may have not understood the reasons behind what had occurred before them, and so they may have misinterpreted what they saw as Jesus being the one who "performed miracles". Yet, the greatest "unseen" miracle was the grounding of the Christ Energy.

Amazingly, Jesus, despite experiencing unimaginable physical and mental pain and torture during his life, reminds us how wonderful a gift our life is;

"Do you listen to the wind?

Do you feel the stars shine upon your hair?

Do you taste the fresh waters?

Do you hold the tiniest of babes?

Do you rejoice in all Creation and feel the energy of light flowing into you?

Do you know peace within your Soul?

This for me was all.

My life was the greatest gift my Father *(God)* gave me."

So, a choice remains; if as a species we continue to separate ourselves from Creation, then we will remain unfulfilled. If however we work in harmony, integrate our light and perfection, then our lives can become truly phenomenal....

I am forever in awe of Creation, Universal flow and God to ignite conversations in the now with a Spirit from the past, enabling us to see how we (as a collective consciousness) have become "stuck". This inertia is restricting the Universal Flow and Creative force that resides within us all, ultimately resulting in a blockage in Creation.

If we give power and live our lives to exaggerated past events, we then unwittingly fuel the untruths of the past.

If, as with Jesus' life, we give reverence to a documented life that is not told in truth, then the result of this false reverence creates layers of unproductive energy which is projected towards that Spirit. The Spirit, as a result of his or her truth being denied, in favor of elaborations, becomes weakened and their individual frequency or spark (that is native to their existence within creation) becomes stifled.

Jesus came to share that "there is no separation". The existence of the spark is required both individually and collectively for the smooth expansion of the Spirit, and for the development of us all as Spirit's (along with the continuing expansion of the rest of the Universes / Creation / God) and our place in this ultimate energy.

For Jesus reminds us; "If each one of you remember in your Spirit you individually contain light and hope, for then you are set free."

All as one, perfectly balanced and "no greater or lesser".

. . . . . .

BOOKS

O is a symbol of the world, of oneness and unity. In different cultures it also means the "eye", symbolizing knowledge and insight. We aim to publish books that are accessible, constructive and that challenge accepted opinion, both that of academia and the "moral majority".

Our books are available in all good English language bookstores worldwide. If you don't see the book on the shelves ask the bookstore to order it for you, quoting the ISBN number and title. Alternatively you can order online (all major online retail sites carry our titles) or contact the distributor in the relevant country, listed on the copyright page.

See our website **www.o-books.net** for a full list of over 400 titles, growing by 100 a year.

And tune in to myspiritradio.com for our book review radio show, hosted by June-Elleni Laine, where you can listen to the authors discussing their books.